# How Can I change?

## VICTORY IN THE STRUGGLE AGAINST SIN

### C.J. Mahaney and Robin Boisvert

**Executive Editor: Greg Somerville**

This life, therefore,
is not righteousness but growth in righteousness,
not health but healing,
not being but becoming,
not rest but exercise.
We are not yet what we shall be, but we are growing toward it;
the process is not yet finished but it is going on.
This is not the end but it is the road;
all does not yet gleam in glory but all is being purified.

— Martin Luther

SOVEREIGN GRACE™ MINISTRIES
The Pursuit *of* Godliness Series

Sovereign Grace Media is a division of Sovereign Grace Ministries, which serves a growing network of local churches in the United States and abroad. For information about the ministry or for permission to reproduce portions of this book, please contact us.

**Sovereign Grace Ministries**
**7505 Muncaster Mill Road**
**Gaithersburg, MD 20877**

**301-330-7400**
**fax: 301-948-7833**
**info@sovgracemin.org**
**www.sovereigngraceministries.org**

Authors: C.J. Mahaney and Robin Boisvert
Cover design: Gallison Design (www.gallisondesign.com)
Book layout: Martin Stanley

ISBN 1-881039-03-X

Printed in the United States of America

0603

# CONTENTS

# HOW TO USE THIS BOOK

*How Can I Change?,* like each book in the Pursuit of Godliness series, is designed for group and individual use. The series is the logical outgrowth of four deeply held convictions:

■ The Bible is our infallible standard for faith, doctrine, and practice. Those who resist its authority will be blown off course by their own feelings and cultural trends.

■ Knowledge without application is lifeless. In order to be transformed, we must apply and practice the truth of God's Word in daily life.

■ Application of these principles is impossible apart from the Holy Spirit. While we must participate in change, he is the source of our power.

■ The church is God's intended context for change. God never intended for us to live isolated from or independent of other Christians. Through committed participation in the local church, we find instruction, encouragement, correction, and opportunities to press on toward maturity in Christ.

As you work through these pages, we trust each of these foundational convictions will be reinforced in your heart.

With the possible exception of the "Group Discussion" questions, the format of this book is equally suited for individuals and small groups. A variety of different elements have been included to make each chapter as interesting and helpful as possible. For those of you who can't get enough of a particular topic, we've listed at the end of each chapter one or more additional books that will help you grow in the Lord.

While you are encouraged to experiment in your use of this book, group discussion will be better served when members work through the material in advance. And remember that you're not going through this book alone. The Holy Spirit is your tutor. With his help, this book has the potential to change your life.

# FOREWORD

When I was a junior in high school, it was required that everyone be timed in a long-distance run. Normally I would have turned in a marginal performance, if that. But this time I decided to put all my effort into the ordeal.

Don't misunderstand—though not an outstanding athlete, I usually held my own, and was willing to work at other sports. But distance running was different. It was hard. Not complex—just hard. It meant pain, and I wasn't into pain. As a matter of fact, during a cross-country unit in gym class, my friends and I, out of sight of our instructor, would regularly jog a shortened course that took us through the high school building, down the hall where the typing classes were held, and out again onto the field. We knocked about a quarter mile off the course that way until the typing teacher got wise to the thundering hoofbeats disturbing his class.

But this time I decided to try my best. So, summoning all my inner fortitude, I pushed myself beyond measure and turned in a remarkable performance. So remarkable, in fact, that the cross-country coach heard about it and tried to recruit me for the team. I responded to him the same way I had when my mother suggested I take ballet lessons along with my sisters: "No thanks."

"But Robin," she said, "boys dance ballet, too."

Not this boy.

I felt like I was going to die at the end of that race, and for obvious reasons. I'd done nothing to train for the race—couldn't be bothered—so I wasn't in shape to persevere.

Twenty-five years later, I've gained a new respect for distance running. It's one of the best analogies for understanding the Christian life, as we see so clearly in Scripture:

> Therefore, since we are surrounded by such a great cloud of witnesses, let us throw off everything that hinders and the sin that so easily entangles, *and let us run with perseverance the race marked out for us.* (Heb 12:1, emphasis added)

This great cloud of witnesses includes those heroic men and women of biblical history—such as Abraham, Joseph, and Moses—who ran their races faithfully (Heb 10).

While there are other helpful illustrations of the Christian life in Scripture, the distance race motif provides much food for thought. Such a race requires perseverance. It requires discipline and training. It requires an eye on the goal. And even though it's not particularly complicated, successful distance runners have been among our more intelligent athletes. They are able to marshal their resources and focus them on the task at hand, one step at a time.

We have written this book for runners—Christian men and women sincerely interested in running the race marked out for them. To those who have tried and failed and are about to give it up as hopeless, we offer encouragement. Having done our share of stumbling along the road, we've consistently found that the One who calls us to run is faithful. His Word and Spirit are available to us. Not only that, but he has a compassionate interest in our success. "A bruised reed he will not break," said the prophet

Isaiah, "and a smoldering wick he will not put out" (Is 42:3). When you are so bent over you're sure you'll snap, when your fire has just about gone out, he is there to revive you.

To those who may feel they have reached a comfortable degree of success in living the Christian life, we offer an exhortation. The prophet warned his hearers, "Woe to those who are at ease in Zion!" (Am 6:1 NAS). Such an attitude is extremely dangerous, for when we think we have a grip on holiness, we are the more inclined to relax and trust in ourselves rather than God. At that point it usually takes a crisis to bring us back to reality.

Finally, this book is for those who simply desire to grow as Christians, who are content in Christ but not satisfied in themselves. Perhaps you're frustrated with your progress. Perhaps you're unsure where to begin. Perhaps you've run for many miles and simply need a second wind. We believe this book will help.

In a day when quick solutions to longstanding problems are too easily offered, we wish to recommend the old paths, having found them tried and true. There is no short course to Christian maturity. There is no crossless way to follow Christ, no instant secret to the Christian life. But like distance running, if the way of the cross is not easy, neither is it complicated. God presents us with a pathway that is narrow yet straight. He makes his ways plain to those who are sincerely interested in following him, and he will show himself strong on behalf of all whose hearts are fully his.

Our goal in introducing the doctrine of sanctification (that's the best we could hope to do in a book this size) is that we might be conformed to the image of Jesus Christ (Ro 8:29). And from the outset we stress the fact that God's Spirit is the One who transforms us (2Co 3:18). Although our vigorous effort is required, all growth is by his grace. With that wonderful truth as our starting block, let us press on toward the mark, each confident that "He who began a good work in you will carry it on to completion until the day of Christ Jesus" (Php 1:6).

— **Robin Boisvert**

*"And we, who with*
*unveiled faces all reflect the Lord's glory,*
*are being transformed into his likeness with ever-increasing glory,*
*which comes from the Lord, who is the Spirit."*

(2 Corinthians 3:18)

CHAPTER ONE

# CAUGHT IN THE GAP TRAP

ROBIN BOISVERT

*Needs:*
*Rope*
*Paper.*
*Tape*
*→ our reality.*

*7 reasons*
*to close*
*the gap*

"All those who are struggling with anger, please come forward. We'd like to pray for you."

It was Sunday morning. I had just finished teaching about anger, and wanted to give the Holy Spirit opportunity to work in the hearts of those present. But I could not have anticipated the response.

About twenty humble saints came down to the front of the auditorium—a large group for a church our size. And yet it wasn't the number that caught my attention. It was the people themselves. Nineteen of the twenty were mothers of young children! (Anger is an occupational hazard, according to most mothers I've ever known.)

As their pastor, I knew all of these women to be serious and dedicated Christians. What caused them to come forward was their intense frustration at being caught in the gap—a gap between the biblical standard of self-control and their own failure to live up to that standard.

Whether the problem is anger, fear, worry, or something as common as laziness, we've all experienced that gap between what we are and what we should be. The Bible says we're new creations, victors, overcomers. And we're not just conquerors—we're *more* than conquerors (Ro 8:37). Sometimes we even feel that way. More often than not, however, we have a hard time seeing beyond our limitations and perpetual failures. And it always seems to be during these seasons of life that Matthew 5:48 surfaces in our Bible reading plan: "Be perfect, therefore, as your heavenly Father is perfect."

Quietly we sigh and think to ourselves, *It will never happen.*

I call this state of mind the "gap trap." Here's how it works: As Christians, we all have a certain amount of knowledge regarding what God expects from us. But we achieve less than we know we should be achieving. There

**For Further Study:**
Even Paul the apostle got caught in the gap trap (Romans 7:21-25). Can you identify with his frustration?

1

exists then a gap between what we know is required and our actual performance. If the distance between what we know and what we're living becomes too great, we can rightly be called hypocrites.

This gap is a fact of Christian life. For most of us, no one need tell us of our inconsistencies—we're all too aware of them. Such awareness should serve to keep us humble and dependent upon God for success. But the trap is often sprung by our ignorance of the doctrine of sanctification. Rather than recognizing that the gap exists to urge us onward in fervent reliance upon Christ, we allow it to condemn us and halt our forward progress. We get trapped into thinking we're just losers, failures, good-for-nothings…and maybe not even Christians. Some even lapse into inaction or disobedience. Those caught in this trap (and, to a certain extent, we all are) suffer unnecessarily from discouragement.

> **"** The Christian life is a matter of becoming in intrinsic character what we already are in Christ…The purpose of these passages (e.g. Romans 6, Colossians 3:5-14, Ephesians 4:22-32) is to show us the great gap between what we are counted or reckoned to be in Christ (justification) and what we are actually in ourselves in daily living (sanctification) in order to urge us to *close the gap*…Paul's purpose is to urge us to become in everyday living what we already are counted to be in Christ.[1] **"**
>
> — **Jay Adams**

*[handwritten margin note: Gap either 1. we allow it to condemn us and halt our forward progress 2. exists to urge us onward in fervent reliance upon Christ.]*

As a pastor, one of my main responsibilities is helping individuals out of the gap trap. I often find myself telling people, "It will not be instant, and it's bound to require serious effort, but getting out of the gap trap is not complicated. And believe me, it will be well worth it."

Perhaps you've found yourself in the gap trap. Maybe you're there right now. If so, we're confident this book can help you close the gap between who you *should* be in Christ and who you *are* in actual practice.

Can you imagine a life in which you are breaking sinful habits and making real progress in godliness? Such a life is possible. And this book is written to assist and encourage you as you make that life your own.

### Between the "Now" and the "Not Yet"

Without question, one of the most frustrating things about the Christian life is the apparent contradiction between what God reckons us to be and what we, by experience, know ourselves to be. Take the Corinthians, for example. At one point Paul assured them, "You were washed, you were sanctified, you were justified in the name of the Lord Jesus Christ and by the Spirit of our God" (1Co 6:11). Sounds like an open-and-shut case, doesn't it? Until you read Paul's second letter to this church, in which he seems to say almost the opposite: "Let us purify ourselves from everything that contaminates body and spirit, perfecting holiness out of reverence for God" (2Co 7:1).

I expect the Corinthians were somewhat confused. Were they sanctified...or contaminated? Actually, they were both, and so are we. In order to explain that, let me take you on a brief tangent.

God's kingdom is both "now" and "not yet." It is present in certain respects and future in others. Our Lord came proclaiming and demonstrating that the kingdom (or rule) of God had intersected human history: "If I drive out demons by the finger of God, then the kingdom of God has come to you" (Lk 11:20). However, God's kingdom has not yet come in its fullness. That won't happen until Jesus returns again in power, when every knee will bow and every tongue will confess that he is Lord. Until then, without denying the present reality of God's kingdom, we fervently pray, "May your kingdom *come*" (Mt 6:10).

**Meditate on 1 John 3:2-3.** What impact should our thoughts about the "not yet" have on the "now"?

*[handwritten notes:]*
*Sry us*
*Sanctified?*
*Contaminated.*
*D-Day*
*VE-Day*

In this respect, God's kingdom closely parallels our individual lives. God, through the wonderful work of justification, has declared us righteous. Our legal standing before him has changed. That issue has been settled once and for all in the high court of heaven. On this side of heaven, though, our internal transformation is an ongoing project. The process of sanctification keeps me busy as a Christian personally, and also provides me with plenty of work as a pastor.

So do we have victory in Jesus or not? Are we overcomers, or are we overcome? Oscar Cullmann suggests an analogy from World War II which I believe can help us grasp this apparent contradiction.[2]

History records two important days toward the end of World War II: D-Day and VE-Day. D-Day took place June 6, 1944 when the Allied forces landed on the beaches of Normandy, France. This was the turning point in the war; once this landing was successfully completed, Hitler's fate was sealed. The war was essentially over. Yet total victory in Europe (VE-Day) did not occur until May 7, 1945 when

German forces surrendered in Berlin. This eleven-month interval is remembered as one of the bloodiest periods of the war. Pitched battles were fought throughout France, Belgium, and Germany. Although the enemy had been mortally wounded, he did not immediately succumb.

The cross was our D-Day. There the Lord Jesus Christ died to break the chains of sin from his people. On the basis of his death and resurrection, we are justified. Yet the final victory awaits Christ's return. There is no doubt as to the outcome of things. But we will still find ourselves involved in skirmishes and battles until the Lord appears in glory to vanquish forever the forces of darkness.

This distinction, if kept in mind, can spare us a lot of discouragement. The battle still rages, but the war has been won. An awareness of Christ's finished work on our behalf is essential for morale as we pursue sanctification. We must study and meditate on the great doctrine of justification until it sinks deeply into our consciousness.

**For Further Study:**
Read 1 Peter 5:8-9. Though God's ultimate triumph is inevitable, we should fight with a healthy respect for our adversary.

## Listerine, Anyone?

Though we are fully justified in Christ (D-Day), we are by no means fully sanctified (VE-Day). Some have failed to understand this.

Bible teacher Ern Baxter tells of an incident that occurred during the Latter Rain Revival of the late 1940s. A heretical teaching had emerged called "the manifest sons of God." It was essentially a doctrine promising total sanctification in this life. In its extreme form, it included the belief that a spiritual elite would receive glorified bodies before Christ's return.

At the close of a meeting where Baxter was preaching, several manifest sons (and daughters) appeared at the rear of the auditorium clad in white robes. When he finished speaking they swept down the aisle to the front of the church and began trying to make disciples to their doctrine of absolute perfection. As he relates the story, "The lady who was their leader was in serious need of Listerine. That's not the kind of perfection I'm looking forward to."[4]

More common than Ern Baxter's scenario are situations

**2** If you were seeking total perfection in this life, which of the following would be hardest for you to do?

❏ Never drive even one mile above the speed limit

❏ Speak with warmth and kindness to every telemarketer who calls

❏ Avoid all unnecessary calories

❏ Never hit the snooze button on your alarm clock

❏ Always pay your income taxes cheerfully

**For Further Study:**
Read Matthew 26:41. When is it safe to assume we've "arrived" at sanctification?

resulting from a shallow, simplistic view of sanctification.

When I was a new believer, I met a young man named Greg, a self-confessed burglar and drug addict who was apparently converted while in prison. Greg's grip on living the Christian life impressed me. He carried himself with a bold certainty and walked with a slight swagger. He talked as if sin were not really a problem for him any longer. More than once he told me how he'd been "saved, sanctified, and filled with the Holy Ghost."

To hear him describe it made it seem so simple. As a new Christian, he'd boarded a train one day, and when he got off hours later he'd had what he termed a "sanctification experience." He assured me that such an experience was a necessary prelude to receiving the baptism in the Holy Spirit, and once that happened, you were all set.

I must admit, there were some things about Greg that didn't seem too sanctified. He had a judgmental streak and a Pharisaical attitude. He could be both overbearing and petty. I recall his indignant remarks when a friend inadvertently set something on top of his Bible: "I beg your pardon—that happens to be the Word of God!" Still, he sure could quote the Bible, and he seemed to understand this business of sanctification.

What a shock when he turned back to selling and using hard drugs.

Greg's problems included an incomplete and therefore incorrect understanding of the Bible's teaching on sanctification. He had done what so many do by focusing only on those favorite Scripture texts which seemed to validate his personal experience.

Sanctification is both *definite* (occurring at conversion) and *progressive*. It didn't all happen in one experience in the past, nor is it to be thought of as only happening by degrees. We *were changed* and we *are changing*. Without dampening the enthusiasm of our successful landing at Normandy, let's be sober and realistic as we assess the opposition lying between us and Berlin. We don't have the option of boarding a

❝ Holiness is not the way to Christ. Christ is the way to holiness.[5] ❞

— **Adrian Rogers**

sanctification train, like Greg claimed to have done. It's going to be a fight every step of the way.

## Worth the Work

For many, "sanctification" is another of those long, theological words often heard but rarely understood. It sounds scholarly and impractical. Yet it is *intensely* practical. The doctrine of sanctification answers questions asked by almost every Christian in Church history:

How do I change?
How do I grow?
How do I become like Christ?
*How do I get out of the gap trap?*

*Signs*

Anything that can answer those questions is worth some effort. Appendix A (page 93) shows how various branches of the Church have handled this issue in the past, but let's see what we can learn about this essential doctrine as it applies to us today.

The biblical meaning of the word *sanctify* is "to set apart; consecrate." (*Holiness* comes from the same Greek root.) It may be applied to a person, place, occasion, or object. When something is sanctified, it is separated from common use and devoted to special use. For instance, in Moses' time, the Day of Atonement was set apart (sanctified) to a holy God. That day became a holy day. A thing sanctified is not made holy simply by being set apart; it derives its holiness from that to which it has been devoted. Because only God is holy, he alone can impart holiness.

Theologically the term "sanctification" has been used to describe the *process* a believer undergoes as the Spirit of God works in him to make him like Christ. The process begins at the

> ❝ Can holiness save us? Can holiness put away sin, make satisfaction for transgressions, pay our debt to God? No, not a whit. God forbid that I should ever say so. Holiness can do none of these things. The brightest saints are all 'unprofitable servants.' Our purest works are not better than filthy rags, when tried by the light of God's holy law. The white robe, which Jesus offers and faith puts on, must be our only righteousness, the name of Christ our only confidence, the Lamb's book of life our only title to heaven. With all our holiness we are no better than sinners. Our best things are stained and tainted with imperfection. They are all more or less incomplete, wrong in the motive or defective in the performance. 'By grace are ye saved through faith; and that not of yourselves, it is the gift of God: not of works, lest any man should boast' (Eph 2:8,9).[6] ❞
>
> — J.C. Ryle

moment we are born again and continues as long as we live. It is marked by daily conflict as we appropriate the grace and strength of God to overcome indwelling sin.

Keep in mind that the *guilt* of sin has already been removed through justification, as Anthony Hoekema explains; sanctification removes the *pollution* of sin:

> By *guilt* we mean the state of deserving condemnation or of being liable to punishment because God's law has been violated. In justification, which is a declarative act of God, the guilt of our sin is removed on the basis of the atoning work of Jesus Christ. By *pollution*, however, we mean the corruption of our nature which is the result of sin and which, in turn, produces further sin. As a result of the Fall of our first parents, we are all born in a state of corruption; the sins which we commit are not only products of that corruption but also add to it. In *sanctification* the pollution of sin is in the process of being removed (though it will not be totally removed until the life to come).[7]

The Bible also describes sanctification as growth in godliness. By godliness I'm referring to a devotion to God and the character that springs from such devotion. Godliness includes a love of God and desire for God.[8] It also includes the fear of God, which John Murray has called the "soul of godliness."[9] Having been delivered from the fear of eternal torment, the Christian fears God by focusing not on his wrath but on his "majesty, holiness and transcendent glory...."[10] The fear of the Lord has a purifying effect on the heart and is a precondition for intimacy with God.

Godliness involves more than morality or zeal. It springs from a union with Christ and a passion to honor him. A godly person wants to be like his Lord so as to give him pleasure. He wants to feel what God feels, think his thoughts after him, and do his will. In short, he wishes to take upon himself the character of God so that God might be glorified. No endeavor is more worthy of our life-long effort: "For physical training is of some value, but godliness has value for all things, holding promise for both the present life and the life to come" (1Ti 4:8).

Both God and man play key roles in the gracious work of sanctification. He, by his amazing grace, initiates our salvation and imparts the desire and power to overcome sin. Responding to and relying on his grace, we then obey the biblical command to "work out your salvation with fear

**For Further Study:**
Do you realize how important and beneficial it is to fear the Lord? (See Psalm 19:9 and 25:14, Proverbs 1:7 and 9:10, and 1 Peter 1:17.)

> **"** Sanctification, says the Westminster Shorter Catechism (Q.35), is 'the work of God's free grace, whereby we are renewed in the whole man after the image of God, and are enabled more and more to die unto sin, and live unto righteousness.' The concept is not of sin being totally eradicated (that is to claim too much) or merely counteracted (that is to say too little), but of a divinely wrought character change freeing us from sinful habits and forming in us Christlike affections, dispositions, and virtues.[11] **"**
>
> — **J.I. Packer**

**Meditate on
1 Timothy 6:11-16.**
Paul would have been a very motivating drill sergeant.

and trembling, for it is God who works in you to will and to act according to his good purpose" (Php 2:12-13).

The New Testament charts a course for holy living which is a middle ground (actually a higher ground) between legalism on one side and license on the other. Those church traditions that have placed the accent too heavily on God's work within us *without* expecting that work to result in a growing desire for godliness, veer off the path toward license. "For, as I have often told you before and now say again even with tears, many live as enemies of the cross of Christ. Their destiny is destruction, their god is their stomach, and their glory is in their shame. Their mind is on earthly things" (Php 3:18-19). On the other hand, there are those who have so emphasized man's part that they elevate technique above God's truth and end in legalism. (There are, of course, varying degrees of these driftings.)

**3** Take this short True/False quiz to see how well you've understood this material so far:

*(Answers printed upside down at bottom of page 9)*

- The word "sanctify" means "to tear apart; desecrate."    T    F

- Sanctification begins the moment you are born again and continues as long as you live.    T    F

- The guilt of our sin has been removed by justification.    T    F

- Godliness refers exclusively to a person's morality and zeal.    T    F

- God has sole responsibility for our sanctification.    T    F

## How to Attain Perfection

One common question I hear Christians raise is, "How far can I expect this process of sanctification to go? Will I ever be completely free from sin?" It's a question that becomes especially relevant when you read a statement like Paul's to the Philippian church: "Let us therefore, *as many as are perfect,* have this attitude; and if in anything you have a different attitude, God will reveal that also to you" (Php 3:15 NAS). Jesus said it even more pointedly in a verse quoted earlier: "Be perfect, therefore, as your heavenly Father is perfect" (Mt 5:48).

Does God really expect us to attain perfection?

A yearning for perfection has inspired many to pursue God. Throughout human history poets and philosophers have expressed the desire to regain a lost innocence and purity. Contemporary songwriters Crosby, Stills, and Nash celebrated the Woodstock experience with a song that said, "We are star dust, we are golden, we are caught in the devil's bargain. And we've got to get ourselves back to the Garden."

The trouble is, we're anything but perfect and we know it. In the make-believe world of movies, Mary Poppins may cheerfully refer to herself as "practically perfect in every way," but it doesn't work like that in real life. And we certainly won't reach perfection via Woodstock.

R.A. Muller points out that Scripture clearly tells us to be perfect, while at the same time giving evidence that perfection is unattainable in this life.[12] This presents us with a dilemma. We are not free to throw up our hands and admit defeat. But neither may we adopt a "can-do" mentality toward perfection which has more in common with positive thinking than with the Bible. The only way to solve this dilemma is by realizing the New Testament views perfection two ways.[13]

> ❝ When the dawn of...God's holiness breaks upon our spirits, we are delivered from all superficial and inadequate thoughts about our own sanctification. We are also preserved from any cheap teaching that encourages us to think that there are shortcuts by which we may more easily obtain holiness. Holiness is not an experience; it is the re-integration of our character, the rebuilding of a ruin. It is skilled labor, a long-term project, demanding everything God has given us for life and godliness.[14] ❞
>
> — Sinclair Ferguson

Paul's vision for the Philippians was *maturity,* not faultlessness. Note how the New International Version translates his comment to the Philippian church: "All of us who are *mature* should take such a view of things" (Php 3:15). The "perfect" in this sense may best be described as "those who have made reasonable progress in spiritual growth and stability."

It's a natural thing for every child to want to be big, to be full-grown. This is no less true of the believer. Rather than take a casual or haphazard approach to growth, we should let the call to perfection urge us onward in a serious quest to be like Jesus. Paul's own example should be the model for us all:

Not that I have already obtained all this, or have already been made perfect, but I press on to take

*Changing the definition of Perfection*

**Meditate on 1 Peter 1:14-16.** Does this command seem unrealistic? Would God ask you to do the impossible?

*Be holy as He is holy.*

Answers: F, T, T, F, F

9

> **❝** We must first be made good before we can do good.[16] **❞**
>
> **— Hugh Latimer**

hold of that for which Christ Jesus took hold of me. Brothers, I do not consider myself yet to have taken hold of it. But one thing I do: Forgetting what is behind and straining toward what is ahead, I press on toward the goal to win the prize for which God has called me heavenward in Christ Jesus. (Php 3:12-14)

**4** A once-popular bumper sticker read, "Christians Aren't Perfect—Just Forgiven." What kind of attitude might this reflect? (Especially if the car is speeding.)

We see a second use of the word perfection in Paul's first letter to the Corinthians. "When perfection comes," he says, "the imperfect disappears" (1Co 13:10). In this sense, perfection is a term rightly restricted to the Godhead—a perfection that will not be seen until Christ returns. Theologian Louis Berkhof prefers to speak of God's *perfections* rather than his attributes.[15] God alone is faultless. No matter how much we mature in this life, we will never reach perfection until that day when God perfects us in glory.

## Seven Reasons to Close the Gap

Generally speaking, the world has a negative impression of holiness. Many equate it with a glum, cross-carrying existence devoid of joy. It is seen more as a "holier-than-thou" self-righteousness than as the joyful experience it really is. As we close, let's refute that idea by looking at some of the many benefits and blessings we gain from following Christ. Here are seven fruits of sanctification:

**God is glorified.** When we are holy, we give weight to our claim that God is as real and wonderful as we say he is. Paul tells us the good works of Christians adorn the doctrine of Christ (Tit 2:10 NAS). Even those who deny God are forced to admit his reality when his people walk in his ways.

**Ongoing fellowship in this life with the Godhead.** "If anyone loves me," said Jesus, "he will obey my teaching. My Father will love him, and we will come to him and make our home with him" (Jn 14:23). It's a tremendous joy and comfort to have the abiding presence of the Father and the Son through the Holy Spirit. And Jesus indicates that this presence is a loving presence, not indifferent or impersonal. Of course, along with his presence comes his power, which enables us to overcome the obstacles of life.

> There is no abiding joy without holiness...How important then is the truth that sanctifies! How crucial is the Word that breaks the power of counterfeit pleasures! And how vigilant we should be to light our paths and load our hearts with the Word of God![17]
> — John Piper

**Fellowship with other Christians.** If we walk in darkness, we can't enjoy authentic relationships with other believers. "But if we walk in the light, as he is in the light, we have fellowship with one another, and the blood of Jesus, his Son, purifies us from all sin" (1Jn 1:7).

The Lord promises to provide us with companions, fellow travelers on the road of sanctification. For my part, I've found that God's truth combined with the example of God's people is absolutely necessary for my spiritual growth. And when I've walked in his ways I've never lacked for either. We need one another in the context of the church in order to succeed. Holiness and Christian community go hand in hand.

**Assurance of salvation.** Though our salvation is not based upon our pursuit of holiness, assurance of salvation is most certainly connected with it. In his second letter, Peter exhorts his readers to make every effort to pile up spiritual virtues, adding goodness to faith and knowledge to goodness until self-control, perseverance, godliness, brotherly kindness, and love are had in abundant measure (2Pe 1:5-9). He warns that when these are lacking, a person may forget...

> ...that he has been cleansed from his past sins. Therefore, my brothers, be all the more eager to make your calling and election sure. For if you do these things, you will never fall, and you will receive a rich welcome into the eternal kingdom of our Lord and Savior Jesus Christ. (2Pe 1:9-11)

**Evangelism.** As a young man under conviction of sin, I tried my best to find fault with Christians so that I might reject their message and dismiss them as hypocrites. But though they weren't perfect, I could find no major inconsistencies. The large family who reached out to me with the gospel made more of an impact on me with their lifestyle than with their words. The husband loved his wife, the wife respected her husband, the children obeyed

11

**Meditate on 1 Peter 2:12.** Though non-Christians may mock your lifestyle now, what effect will it ultimately have on them?

their parents, and they were all joyful. I had never seen anything like it.

It has been said that while the world may not read its Bible, it certainly does read its Christians. God uses holy people to reach others. Not perfect, but holy.

**Understanding, wisdom, and knowledge.** These treasures are laid up for those who seek God wholeheartedly (Pr 2:1-11). They are withheld from the scorner, the rebel, and the fool.

**Seeing God.** Scripture tells us, "Make every effort to live in peace with all men and to be holy; without holiness no one will see the Lord" (Heb 12:14). While the full meaning of this passage is shrouded in mystery, Scripture does have much to say about "the beatific vision," or seeing God. It will occur following our Lord's return when every enemy has been vanquished and we have been totally sanctified. At that time our vision of God will be continual and intense, without distraction or the self-consciousness caused by sin. Then we shall know even as we are known. Not that our knowledge of God will be complete, for he will be ever revealing more and more of his infinite and wonderful self to us.

> Blessed are the pure in heart, for they will see God.
>
> — Jesus (Matthew 5:8)

"Blessed are the pure in heart," Jesus said, "for they will see God" (Mt 5:8). This ongoing illumination of his greatness and goodness is by far the most outstanding wonder to result from a life of holiness.

As you can see, there are plenty of good reasons to close the gap between God's expectations of us and our own experience. We were made to share in his holiness—not just in heaven, but here on earth. Step by step, we can learn to overcome sin and live in a way that increasingly reflects the glory and character of God.

In this first chapter, we have attempted to whet your appetite for godliness. Beginning with Chapter Two, we'll start building the biblical framework necessary to support a holy—and happy—life. ■

1. What kind of symptoms indicate that one is caught in the "gap trap"?

2. A certain gap between God's standards and our performance is unavoidable; too much, though, and we qualify as hypocrites. Where do we draw the line?

3. How is our sanctification both past history and future hope?

4. The fear of the Lord, says the author, is a "precondition for intimacy with God." (Page 7) What does he mean?

5. To what extent should a mature Christian be free of sin?

6. Now that you have finished this chapter, how would you explain Matthew 5:48 to a brand-new Christian?

*How to Help People Change* by Jay E. Adams (Grand Rapids, MI: Zondervan Publishing House, 1986)

*Saved by Grace* by Anthony A. Hoekema (Grand Rapids, MI: Eerdmans Publishing Co., 1989)

CHAPTER TWO

# WHERE IT ALL BEGINS

C.J. MAHANEY

Not many years ago the rumor began circulating that a
popular rock star had been "born again." Reaction
from the Christian community was predictably enthusias-
tic. But when he learned of his alleged conversion, the
rock star quickly put an end to the rumor: "It was report-
ed that I was born again. That's not true. What I said was
that I was into *porn* again."

One little letter can make quite a difference.

I find myself skeptical when I hear that public figures
have been converted. Even if the individual does acknowl-
edge a commitment to follow Christ, his or her lifestyle
rarely seems to reflect a corresponding change. There is
often no evidence of repentance. There is no involvement
in a local church. As ordinary citizen Joe Six-Pack observes
this apparent contradiction, he inaccurately concludes
that this is what it means to be born again.

Charles Colson is a notable exception to the pattern. A
former attorney and presidential aide in the Nixon admin-
istration, Colson was convicted and imprisoned for his
role in Watergate. It seemed suspicious when, during this
period, he claimed to have submitted his life to Christ.
But this was no scheme for reducing his sentence. Colson's
conversion was genuine, as evidenced by his new lifestyle.
His book *Born Again* gives an eloquent and powerful
account of his authentic encounter with the gospel.

Although the phrase "born again" is commonly used in
today's culture, its theological implications have been
obscured. For example, when retired heavyweight boxer
George Foreman returned to the ring, sportscasters spoke
of his career being "born again." Politicians who experience a setback and then regain popularity are sometimes
referred to as born again. And many people think of born-
again Christians as a hyperactive fringe group within the
Church, unaware that the new birth is a biblical prerequi-

**Meditate on 1 Peter
2:2-3.** What is the
"milk" described here?
Why is pure milk
essential for spiritual
growth?

15

> **“** Becoming a Christian is not making a new start in life; it is receiving a new life to start with.[1] **”**
>
> **— Thomas Adams**

site for being a part of the Church at all!

Even the mature Christian can fail to understand this critical phrase. Yet if we ever hope to change as God intends, we must begin with an understanding and experience of regeneration—the new birth. Here's where the whole process of sanctification begins.

**1** Which of the following phrases best describes, in your opinion, what it means to be born again?

*(Answer is printed upside down at bottom of page)*

- ❑ Making a decision to start living a better life
- ❑ Renewing a long-lost commitment to Christ
- ❑ Asking God to forgive your sins and live in your heart
- ❑ Telling all your former friends they're going to Hell
- ❑ None of the above

## The Education of a Pharisee

The phrase "born again" didn't originate with President Jimmy Carter. It originated with Jesus Christ. Let's discover where he introduced it and how he meant it to be understood as we eavesdrop on a brain-bending conversation in the third chapter of John.

Nicodemus was a Pharisee and a member of the Jewish ruling council, the Sanhedrin. He commanded great respect in Jerusalem as a theologian and teacher of the law. In light of his position and prestige, it's surprising that Nicodemus would pay a private visit to Jesus. After all, Jesus lacked the formal training Nicodemus and his peers valued so highly. Besides, this blue-collar rabbi had just wreaked havoc in the Temple and insinuated he had unique authority from God (Jn 2:13-22). But Nicodemus was intrigued by Jesus' teaching, and he could not deny or dismiss the miracles taking place. So, with a certain degree of humility, the prominent religious insider called on the uneducated carpenter from Galilee:

> Rabbi, we know you are a teacher who has come from God. For no one could perform the miraculous signs you are doing if God were not with him. (Jn 3:2)

One thing could be said for the Pharisees—they knew the importance of etiquette. By addressing Jesus as "Rabbi," Nicodemus was expressing respect for his status as a teacher and a willingness to learn. But his next statement was one he would quickly regret: "Rabbi, we know...."

Answer: None of the above. For a biblical definition, read on.

Not the recommended way to begin a conversation with the Son of God.

Jesus could have confronted Nicodemus for his arrogant attitude and ended the conversation there. Instead, he chose to help Nicodemus see how limited his knowledge really was. His method? A quick game of Biblical Jeopardy. Category: Regeneration, for $200.

"I tell you the truth," Jesus replied, "no one can see the kingdom of God unless he is born again" (vs. 3).

The Lord's statement perplexed Nicodemus. "How can a man be born when he is old?" he asked. "Surely he cannot enter a second time into his mother's womb to be born!" Nicodemus could not comprehend what Jesus meant, nor was he accustomed to being addressed this way. It was typically his place to give the answers, not grope for them. He may even have been in the Temple when Jesus, as a 12-year-old boy, amazed the priests with his questions. But Jesus was no longer an adolescent.

"I tell you the truth," Jesus continued, "no one can enter the kingdom of God unless he is born of water and the Spirit...You should not be surprised at my saying, 'You must be born again'" (vs. 5,7).

But Nicodemus was surprised. In fact, he was shocked. "How can this be?" he asked.

At this point Nicodemus needed two Tylenol. Adding to his difficulty was a sense of humiliation, especially when Jesus said, "I tell you the truth, *we speak of what we know,* and we testify to what we have seen, but still you people do not accept our testimony. I have spoken to you of earthly things and you do not believe; how then will you believe if I speak of heavenly things?" (vs. 11-12).

It's easy to look down on the humbled scholar, but let's subject ourselves to the same examination: Do we understand what Jesus was saying about being born again? Are we surprised at Jesus' statements? Unless we've reached the place where, like Nicodemus, we

> ❝ We rarely take this teaching [that man cannot enter the kingdom of God] sufficiently seriously, perhaps because it cuts from under our feet the last vestiges of our natural self-sufficiency. It highlights the biblical teaching that our salvation is all of grace. The one thing necessary is the one thing we ourselves cannot perform![2] ❞
>
> — Sinclair Ferguson

**For Further Study:**
Read Matthew 19:23-26. What are the odds, apart from God's intervention, of a person entering the kingdom of God?

> ❝ The new birth is not only a mystery that no man understands, it is a miracle that no man can undertake.[3] ❞
>
> — Richard Baxter

*You*

*must*

*be born*

*again*

**For Further Study:**
How does Abraham's fathering of Isaac and Ishmael show the contrast between our efforts and God's? (See Genesis 21:1-13 and Romans 9:6-9)

ask "How can this be?", it's unlikely we have fully understood the mystery and miracle of regeneration.

## Nothing to Contribute

What Jesus intentionally omitted was any suggestion that Nicodemus was personally responsible for being born again. In fact, he said the opposite: "Flesh gives birth to flesh, but the Spirit gives birth to spirit" (Jn 3:6).

It's not hard to see why Nicodemus would find Christ's comments so confusing. Having misunderstood and misinterpreted the law, the Pharisees sought to establish their own righteousness before God. Nicodemus would have assumed that being born again (whatever that meant) involved some effort or contribution on his part. Most of us would assume the same. And it is exactly that assumption Jesus was challenging.

"You must be born again" is not a command to believe in Christ; it is a statement clarifying what *he* must do in us. "Regeneration is a change wrought in us by God," writes C. Samuel Storms, "not an autonomous act performed by us for ourselves."[4]

Pause a moment to consider the staggering implications of Christ's words:

■ Though absolutely essential to the Christian life, regeneration cannot be achieved by human effort.

■ God is the sole author of the new birth; it is not a cooperative effort.

■ Regeneration is an experience we must have but only God can provide.

It's not because Nicodemus lacked intelligence that he found the Lord's words so perplexing; it's because they required a paradigm shift in his thinking. They revealed how helpless and dependent he was on the mercy of God.

Before we continue, let me clarify one point. I'm not minimizing the importance of repentance and faith. These must characterize our response to regeneration, and they are essential to conversion and our ongoing sanctification. But from my perspective they are the result of the new birth, not the cause. Theologian A.A. Hodge cautions us to maintain Scripture's perspective: "Whatever man may do after regeneration, the first quickening of the dead must originate with God."[6]

Consider this carefully. Appreciate what a radical transformation is required, and how incapable and impotent you are to produce it. Regeneration is the distinct work of God alone. As J.I. Packer says, "It is not a change which man does anything to bring about, any more than infants do anything to induce, or contribute to, their own procreation and birth."[7] We are not born "of human decision ...but born of God" wrote John (Jn 1:13).

A new, righteous nature has been imparted, of which God is the sole author. In addition, we have the assurance that "he who began a good work in you [regeneration] will carry it on to completion until the day of Christ Jesus" (Php 1:6). That should produce some serious rejoicing!

We no longer need to worry whether our will power and self-discipline are sufficient. They're not. Being conformed to the image of Christ is not ultimately dependent on our ability. Rather, we can be confident concerning our growth in godliness because of God's definitive work. He has put within us a new disposition, a passion for righteousness. "This," says J. Rodman Williams, "is the greatest miracle that any person can ever experience."[8]

**Meditate on Titus 3:4-7.**
Recognizing the source of our salvation (v.5) strengthens our hope for eternal life (v.7).

## Let There Be Life

What actually occurs when one is born again?

J.I. Packer says the word regeneration "denotes a new beginning of life...it speaks of a creative renovation wrought by the power of God."[9] When God regenerated you, he called into being something that did not previously exist. The Bible describes it this way: "For God, who said, 'Let light shine out of darkness,' made his light shine in our hearts to give us the light of the knowledge of the glory of God in the face of Christ" (2Co 4:6). The parallel here between our regeneration and creation is intentional. Our regeneration was no less a creative act of God. The same God who said, "Let there be light" spoke to us one day and said, "Let there be life." *And there was life!*

The new birth can also be viewed as a resurrection. Though we were dead in sin and were incapable of altering this condition, we have now been made alive to God by the regenerating work of the Holy Spirit. Theologian R.C. Sproul explains this in greater detail:

> The Spirit recreates the human heart, quickening it from spiritual death to spiritual life. Regenerate people are new creations. Where formerly they had no disposition, inclination, or desire for the things of God, now they are disposed and inclined toward God. In regeneration, God plants a desire for himself in the human heart that otherwise would not be there.[10]

"A dead man cannot assist in his own resurrection," observes W.G.T. Shedd.[11] Had it not been for the gracious work of the Holy Spirit, who gave us a new life complete with a new nature and a new desire to please, serve, obey, and glorify God, we would still be spiritually dead and hostile to God.

Regeneration is distinct from other facets of our salvation. For example, while justification alters our legal status before God (that is, we are declared righteous rather than guilty), regeneration transforms our fundamental nature. This internal change is so radical and extensive that we are now described as new creations. The image of God corrupted at the fall is recreated through the new birth and progressively renewed through sanctification. But unlike sanctification, regeneration is not a process. It does not take place gradually or by degrees. It is a sovereign and *instantaneous* work of God in our lives.

Please don't misunderstand me. Not everyone is regenerated with all the dramatic experiences Paul had. Here is

**Meditate on 1 Peter 1:23.** How does this analogy add to your understanding of the new birth?

**3** Here's the situation: You are a youth specialist who counsels kids with a rare mental disorder—They are absolutely convinced they gave birth to themselves. What kind of anxieties would you expect this to produce in them?

(Would you expect to see similar anxieties in Christians who don't understand God's role in regeneration?)

a man who was supernaturally blinded for three days and audibly addressed from heaven. Yet Paul wasn't the only person born again in the Book of Acts. When Lydia heard the gospel at a women's prayer meeting, "The Lord opened her heart to respond to Paul's message" (Ac 16:14). That's all there was to it. Paul's eyes were temporarily blinded, and Lydia's heart was quietly opened. Different experiences, yet the result was exactly the same.

> ** " Regeneration is a change which is known and felt: known by works of holiness and felt by a gracious experience.[12] "**
>
> — **Charles H. Spurgeon**

Often we are tempted to measure the authenticity of a conversion by the experiences accompanying it. Everyone enjoys hearing about the gang leader or drug dealer whose life is dramatically changed. But suppose you're a Lydia. You were just driving along in the car one day, listening to a tape somebody had loaned you, and with nobody to witness it God gently opened up your heart. You didn't hear any voices, the car didn't swerve off the road. Nothing dramatic. But by the time you got to work you knew, even if you couldn't explain it, that something significant had happened. You were different. You had been born again.

**For Further Study:**
Who is "the one who makes men holy"? (Hebrews 2:11) For what stages of our sanctification is he responsible? (Hebrews 12:2)

I've had the privilege of visiting the spot in England where John Wesley was born again. Consider his simple account of that moment: "I felt my heart strangely warmed within me." Hardly what one would describe as an explosive experience, and yet the validity and impact of Wesley's regeneration is undeniable.

**4** In the space below, or at the bottom of this page, draw a simple timeline of your life, starting at birth and extending to the present. Then indicate when you experienced each of the following: regeneration, justification, sanctification, repentance, and faith. Which happened at a specific point in time? Which are ongoing?

Whether discreet or dramatic, each new birth has this in common: it has been exclusively and entirely authored by God. The plot and the characters are unique, but the story line is always the same. We are new creations. The old has gone, the new has come.

## A Futile Resolution

It's not only in his gospel that we find John including remarkable statements about regeneration. Let's close by looking at these startling words:

No one who is born of God will continue to sin, because God's seed remains in him; he cannot go on sinning, because he has been born of God. (1Jn 3:9)

Have you ever read this verse and been confused? It can't possibly mean what it says...can it? Few people can exist even an hour or two without sinning in some way or another. Perhaps the real meaning of the verse got lost in translation. On the other hand, we worry, *What if it is accurate? That doesn't seem to be my experience...Does this mean I haven't been "born of God"?*

John isn't implying that real Christians are *incapable* of sinning. That's evident from the first chapter of this same letter, where he wrote, "If we claim to be without sin, we deceive ourselves and the truth is not in us" (1Jn 1:8). No—sin is still very much present, and though its dominion over our lives has been destroyed, we could yield to its influence at any time. But in writing that those born of God "cannot go on sinning," John shows that regeneration has made us incapable of *continuing to sin.*

John's meaning in this passage, according to Anthony Hoekema, is that the Christian "does not keep on doing and enjoying sin, with complete abandon...[H]e or she is not able to keep on sinning with enjoyment, to keep on living in sin."[14] John R.W. Stott sums it up more simply: "The believer may fall into sin, but he will not walk in it."[15]

Do you see the difference?

Suppose I were foolish enough to test John's assertion by making this personal resolution: "In the next six months I will seek to develop a lifestyle of sin." This obviously is not something I would desire or recommend. However, I don't believe I would be able to carry out such a resolution. Why? Because I have been born of God. I now have a new heart, a new life, and a new inclination to pursue righteousness and please God. Though I still commit sins, because of his regenerating power I am incapable of devoting myself to sin or continuing in it. I will never again be able to enjoy sin as a lifestyle. Only a divine act could have accomplished this.

> **❝** Regeneration occurs primarily in the central area of man's being, namely, his heart or spirit. In this deepest level of human existence there is a decisive change.[13] **❞**
>
> — **J. Rodman Williams**

No longer are we helpless or defenseless in our daily confrontation with sin. We are not destined to walk in continual disobedience and defeat. God has internally,

**Meditate on Ephesians 4:22-24.** What characterizes the "new self" we have become through regeneration?

supernaturally, and fundamentally transformed us. We now possess the desire and ability to please him for the rest of our lives. Motivated and empowered by grace, we can anticipate a lifetime of progressive and definitive change.

This is where sanctification begins—in the security and confidence that we have been born again, not by our own effort but by the power and purpose of God. ■

**GROUP DISCUSSION**

1. What are some words that a non-Christian might use to describe a typical "born again" Christian?

2. What is one possible reason celebrity conversions are so frequently superficial?

3. Thomas Adams has written, "Take away the mystery from the new birth and you have taken away its majesty."[16] What makes regeneration mysterious?

4. Is it a struggle for you to believe that God was solely responsible for your rebirth?

5. If Lydia and Paul represent the extremes of the born again experience, where would you be on the spectrum?

6. Discuss the timeline you sketched on page 21. Any questions about the sequence of salvation?

7. Read Hebrews 12:2. How does this "unconditional guarantee" affect your view of sanctification?

8. Has this chapter prompted you to think differently about the new birth?

**RECOMMENDED READING**

*The Christian Life* by Sinclair Ferguson (Carlisle, PA: The Banner of Truth Trust, 1989)

*God's Words* by J.I. Packer (Downers Grove, IL: InterVarsity Press, 1981)

# CHAPTER THREE

# UNITED WITH CHRIST

ROBIN BOISVERT

When I was converted in 1972, in the wake of the charismatic and Jesus movements, I wasn't impressed by logical arguments about God or the Christian life. Mine was an irreverent generation, a "get high and stay high" generation. I was more likely to mock any serious conversation on the subject of religion than listen.

What I needed was an experience with God. And that is exactly what I got.

I met a Christian family whose joyful lives made a tremendous impression on me. They talked about Jesus as if he were right there, and they acted as if his life made a real difference to them. At first I thought it was quaint. But then I became curious. I was attracted by the quality of their lives. And when they explained that it had not always been this way for them, but that Jesus had changed their lives, I began to hope the same could be true for me.

**Meditate on 2 Timothy 3:16-17.** If you're serious about change, here's the ticket.

By "changed life" I am referring to the difference Jesus Christ makes in a person's manner, habits, and worldview, even down to the very core of his nature. This family was solid proof that God did indeed make a difference. And when I was born again and my life began to change, I too concluded that Jesus is alive.

But I also learned that change involves more than a one-time experience. We need to understand how change happens, why it happens, and who makes it happen. These issues are squarely addressed in Scripture. Here's where to go if you want to grow.

## A Letter to Rome

How do we overcome sin and live victoriously in Christ? Christians everywhere are looking for answers to this question...many of them in the wrong places. As you might expect, God has given the answer in his Word. The sixth chapter of Paul's letter to the church at Rome has long been recognized for its essential contribution to the doctrine of sanctification. In it we find Paul contending for a proper understanding of what it means to live as a Christian. But it would be a mistake to try to discover Paul's meaning in Romans 6 without regard for its context, so a brief review of the letter is in order.

Romans, more than any of Paul's other letters, systematically sets out the doctrine of salvation. After some introductory remarks, he unleashes a stinging indictment of the entire human race, showing that all men are guilty as sinners before God. He then explains how God justifies those sinners through faith in Jesus Christ. This is the gist of the first four chapters.

In Chapter 5 Paul begins to talk about the peace and assurance that come to us as a direct result of Christ's atoning work on the cross. We now have peace with God and can rejoice in the hope of the glory of God. We can even rejoice in tribulations that come our way because they develop our character and produce hope. God's love has been poured out upon us through the Holy Spirit. And since these great things were done for us when we were his enemies, we can be all the more assured of God's continued grace now that we're his friends.

In the latter part of Chapter 5 Paul sketches a comparison and contrast between Jesus and Adam, showing that the sacrifice of Christ more than compensates for the misery caused by Adam's sin. He ends the chapter with these two verses:

**For Further Study:**
Paul's opponents convinced the church in Galatia that his message trivialized the Law. See how strongly Paul responds in Galatians 1:6-9 and 3:1-14.

The law was added so that the trespass might increase. *But where sin increased, grace increased all the more,* so that, just as sin reigned in death, so also grace might reign through righteousness to bring eternal life through Jesus Christ our Lord. (Ro 5:20-21, emphasis added)

Paul would like to go on describing the blessings of justification, but he pauses, realizing his last statement could easily be misinterpreted. Thus he begins Chapter 6 with a frontal assault on those who would try to twist his meaning:[1] "What shall we say, then? Shall we go on sinning so that grace may increase? By no means! We died to sin; how can we live in it any longer?" (Ro 6:2).

When rightly preached, the gospel of grace will always be open to the charge that it promotes lawlessness. Wherever Paul went he was hounded by opponents who accused him of teaching people that since they were forgiven, it did not matter how they lived. This was how they distorted his reasoning: "If God forgives us freely by grace (which he does) and if it is true that God's grace is magnified in the forgiving of sin (which it is), then why not sin all the more so that more grace flows and God receives more glory?"

"Not so fast." says Paul. "You're missing something fundamental. Through this gospel, we *died* to sin. And if that's the case, how can we go on living in it?"

Paul spends the rest of Chapter 6 countering this charge of lawlessness, or antinomianism. In doing so, he not only answers his critics but supplies us with some of the richest teaching to be found in the New Testament. For here we discover what it means to be united with Christ, a status that radically alters our relationship to sin.

## Were You There?

We can all look back on individuals who have influenced our lives: our parents, a special friend, or perhaps an effective elementary school teacher. But Jesus Christ is different from any other. It's certainly true that many who have never been born again have been influenced by our Lord's example and teaching, but the New Testament has always held that real faith in Jesus Christ leads to a relationship much more penetrating and infinitely more significant than mere moral influence. Paul talks about our being "in Christ" and Christ being "in us." And the implications of this mysterious union are, without any exaggeration, astounding.

John R.W. Stott has written,

> The great theme of Romans 6, and in particular verses 1-11, is that the death and resurrection of Jesus Christ are not only historical facts and significant doctrines, but personal experiences of the Christian believer. They are events in which we ourselves have come to share. All Christians have been

**For Further Study:** Colossians 3:3 says "your life is now hidden with Christ in God." That brings tremendous security—a truth David captures beautifully in Psalm 91.

27

united to Christ in his death and resurrection. Further, if this is true, if we have died with Christ and risen with Christ, it is inconceivable that we should go on living in sin.[2]

**2** If you could share in the accomplishments of one of these famous individuals, who would it be?

❑ Martin Luther King, Jr.: Civil rights leader

❑ Winston Churchill: British politician

❑ Thomas Edison: Prolific inventor

❑ Beverly Sills: Opera singer

❑ Michael Jordan: Basketball legend

❑ Madame Curie: First person to win two Nobel prizes

❑ Jesus Christ: Creator, Savior, and Lord

Below are the verses from Romans chapter six that highlight our union with Christ:

Or don't you know that all of us who were baptized into Christ Jesus were baptized into his death? We were therefore buried *with him* through baptism into death in order that, just as Christ was raised from the dead through the glory of the Father, we too may live a new life. If we have been united *with him* like this in his death, we will certainly also be united *with him* in his resurrection. For we know that our old self was crucified *with him* so that the body of sin might be done away with, that we should no longer be slaves to sin. (Ro 6:3-6, emphasis added)

That our Lord actually conquered death is an overwhelming truth. Yet, as amazing as this is, it is perhaps more remarkable that *we* are considered as being united with him in his death, burial, and resurrection. Paul reiterates this truth in another letter:

*I* have been crucified *with Christ* and I no longer live, but Christ lives *in me*. The life I live in the body, I live by faith in the Son of God, who loved me and gave himself for me. (Gal 2:20, emphasis added)

Note the phrases "with Christ" and "in me" in the passages above. They point to our union with Jesus Christ. Paul uses the act of baptism to remind us of these truths. What he is eager to show, however, is not baptism, but the faith that leads to baptism. It's upon this faith that our present union with Christ is built.

So what are the implications of this relationship? Somehow we are connected to Jesus Christ himself. And this is one of those cases where *who* you know is a lot more important than what you know—a lesson I learned in a Connecticut deli.

**For Further Study:**
Note the places in John 17 where Jesus refers to being "in" his disciples and vice versa (vs. 21, 23, and 26).

In 1974 my younger sister Joyce and I visited our aging grandmother in Bridgeport, Connecticut. One day Joyce suggested we go across the street to the deli and get some subs. But Grandma's neighborhood had been deteriorating, and as soon as we walked in I knew we had made a big mistake. The place was packed with hardened, menacing-looking teenagers. Things got quiet as all eyes fixed on us—and no one was smiling.

A number of thoughts crossed my mind. *Do they think we're invading their turf? I wonder if they're old enough to know you can get in trouble for murder?*

I still get nervous thinking about it. Joyce, on the other hand, was cool as a cucumber. Although attractive and very feminine, she had spent a couple of years as a director at a Job Corps training camp in Montana where she gained valuable experience handling punks. And in future years she would go on to serve as a public health nurse in Alaska, hike much of the Appalachian Trail, and work as a shock trauma nurse. (These are just the highlights.) I guess you could say she was fearless.

But not I. As we stood there, surrounded by imminent danger, Joyce sensed my apprehension. She said in a voice I thought much too loud, "What's the matter? You scared?"

I didn't feel like answering, at least not then.

We somehow managed to get our subs and left a few minutes later without incident. Safely outside, I said to her, "Joyce, this is a dangerous part of town. I'm glad you're with me. I need the protection."

It's not what you know, but *who* you know that counts.

> ❝ How can a person who lived nearly two thousand years ago radically change a human life here and now?...Does the Jesus of the past become, in fact, the Jesus of the present? The Apostle Paul says that he does. And this is the difference between his influence and that of any other influential person. He touches us here and now, not merely by the ripples of the historical currents he once set in motion, *but by entering into union with us personally* (emphasis added).[3] ❞
>
> — Lewis Smedes

## The Meaning of Union

**Meditate on Ephesians 4:7-8.** What better captivity than to be hostages of Christ Jesus.

All Christians—not just the spiritual elite—are united with Jesus Christ. If one is not united to Christ, he is not a Christian.[4]

Our union with Christ is a living relationship that provides us with the grace to overcome sin and live victorious lives. Jesus is the author and finisher of our faith, the captain of our salvation. He is the pioneer who has gone before us and has even conquered death. Sinclair Ferguson describes him as the lead climber of a team scaling the holy mountain of Zion. We're roped to him. And just as surely as he has triumphed, so will we.[5]

**3** Meditate on the following biblical facts. Which of these encourages you most?

❑ "I am with you and will watch over you wherever you go" (Ge 28:15)

❑ "Surely I am with you always, to the very end of the age" (Mt 28:20)

❑ "Neither death nor life, nor angels nor demons...will be able to separate us from the love of God that is in Christ Jesus our Lord" (Ro 8:38-39)

❑ "Never will I leave you; never will I forsake you" (Heb 13:5)

This relationship can also be seen in the imagery our Lord himself uses when he says, "I am the vine; you are the branches" (Jn 15:5). We are told to abide in him, for apart from him we can do nothing. The King James Version brings this out as well: "For if we have been *planted together* in the likeness of his death, we shall be also [in the likeness] of [his] resurrection..." (Ro 6:5 KJV, emphasis added). Our union with Christ is dynamic, not static. He has grafted us into a *growing* relationship.

**Meditate on Philippians 2:1.**
Though our union with Christ is a fact, the awareness of that fact should generate plenty of feeling.

Whether or not we *feel* united with Christ is of secondary importance; the fact is, we are. This is our status as believers. Does a marriage cease to exist just because a husband and wife feel distant from each other? Of course not. They remain legally united even if their affections grow cool for a season. Feelings—or the lack thereof—in no way jeopardize the fact of our union with Jesus.

Marriage offers a beautiful analogy of our bond with Christ. In marriage, two people come together to form a new entity, a union. They retain their individual identities while merging in a way that is unique and mysterious. The woman takes the name of her husband, showing her submission to him. The husband assumes responsibility for his wife's support and protection. They hold all assets and liabilities in common, and wear rings as symbolic evidence of their special relationship.

So it is when we are wed to Jesus Christ. Though we retain our own personalities, our natures are dramatically changed as we become partakers of the divine nature. We are no longer the same people we were before. We belong to Christ, having taken his name. We have identified ourselves with him, desiring to be known as his, no matter the cost. We bring all our assets and liabilities into the relationship and so does he. (What an apparently bad deal for the Lord—he gets our sin and we get his righteousness!)

And lastly, baptism is the "wedding ring" which tells a watching world we belong to him.

Our union with Christ is an enduring and eternal union. Jesus reassured his disciples with the promise, "You also may be where I am" (Jn 14:3). The clear meaning is that we will one day enjoy the Lord's physical presence, just as we enjoy his spiritual presence now.

That the Christian is united to Jesus Christ is a clear fact. But just *how* we are united to him is a matter of deep mystery. We know this is effected by the Holy Spirit. To quote Lewis Smedes:

> The Spirit is the living bond between him and us.
> He takes what is Christ's and brings it "down" to us.
> The Spirit is always pictured in personal terms. He
> is not like a pipeline through which some stuff
> called life is poured into us at the other end. He is
> always a living, dynamic creator of life; he brings us
> to our spiritual senses, opens our eyes to the reality
> of Christ, nourishes our faith, disciplines us, and,
> above all, engrafts us into the living Christ.[6]

We haven't been eliminated in this union, but Christ has been added. We haven't been eliminated, but we have been changed by the Spirit who has taken up residence within us. Furthermore, we haven't been handed a guide-book and told to find our way to heaven. Instead, we've been given a Guide who will escort us there personally.

## Shall We Continue in Sin?

As we noted above, Paul answers this question with a resounding negative. We cannot continue in sin, he argues, because "we died to sin." Unfortunately, this phrase has been subject to misinterpretation, sometimes with catastrophic results.

One popular Bible teacher takes Paul's statement to mean sin no longer has any pull on the Christian. He poses this question: If you took a dead man and propped him against the wall, then paraded before him some scantily clad women, what effect would it have on him? No effect at all. Why? Because he's dead. Sin can no longer entice him.

Though certainly appealing, this interpretation contradicts human experience and renders unintelligible the multitude of biblical warnings to avoid sin. Paul urges us not to yield our bodies to sin (Ro 6:12-14), an admonition

**For Further Study:**
Read John 14:19.
"Because I live," says Jesus, "you also will live." What a promise!

**Meditate on Hebrews 4:14-16.** Since Christ himself was tempted "in every way, just as we are," wouldn't it be foolish to pretend we're not?

"entirely gratuitous if we had so died to sin that we were now unresponsive to it."[8] Those who think they are somehow beyond temptation ignore the apostle's warning to the Corinthians: "So, if you think you are standing firm, be careful that you don't fall!" (1Co 10:12).

Some have tried to understand Paul's phrase "we died to sin" as an imperative, a command, something the Christian must perform. The next step is to insist that every Christian have a "death to sin" or "death to self" experience: "You need to die to self. And if it hasn't happened, you need to reckon it to be so until it does."

If we see "dying to sin" as something we must perform, we're headed toward serious discouragement...or worse. I believe this is why many seem to fall so suddenly. (Remember my friend Greg?) They struggle to maintain an outward appearance of victory while on the inside their lives are a mass of frustration. Then when they finally run out of gas, they have no hope for trying again. Having already given it their best shot, they don't see how they can possibly make it.

> ❝ If you consider yourselves to have died in his death, and risen to a new way of life in his resurrection, sin will dominate you no more. You now live under a regime of grace, and grace does not stimulate sin, as law does; grace liberates from sin and enables you to triumph over it.[7] ❞
>
> — F.F. Bruce

I think Sinclair Ferguson has the more accurate interpretation of this death to sin. He writes, "Paul is not telling us to do something; he is analyzing something that has taken place."[9] Despite our ongoing vulnerability to sin's enticement, two things can be said with certainty for those who have been united with Christ:

**We died to the penalty (or guilt) of sin.** Scripture states clearly that "the wages of sin is death" (Ro 6:23). Death is the penalty for sin. Yet our Lord's death eliminated sin's penalty. And because we are "in him," we too have died to the penalty of sin. Another way of saying this is, "Therefore, there is now no condemnation for those who are in Christ Jesus" (Ro 8:1).

**We died to the reign of sin.** As a result of our union with Christ in his death, we are no longer obligated to sin. This is exciting! It's not that we're not *able* to sin but that we're able *not* to sin. Paul says, "For sin shall not be your master, because you are not under law, but under grace" (Ro 6:14).

**Meditate on Romans 6:18.** Commit this one verse to memory and your spiritual "fire-power" will increase immediately.

Slavery is a prominent theme in Romans 6, where two very different types of slavery are presented. Before

32

**4** Indicate which of the following statements are true and which are false.

*(Answers printed upside down at the bottom of this page)*

- Every Christian needs to have a
  "death to self" experience    **T**   **F**

- A truly mature Christian is no
  longer enticed by sin    **T**   **F**

- The sanctified Christian doesn't
  struggle with major temptation    **T**   **F**

- Because I'm dead "in Christ,"
  sin's penalty cannot harm me    **T**   **F**

becoming Christians we were slaves of sin. We had no choice but to sin. Now that we are in Christ we are slaves of God. The master/slave relationship we had with sin has been broken. God is now our master. It is therefore correct to say, "I don't have to serve sin today. I have been set free." But the only person who may truly say this is the person who is God's bondslave.

Though we have died with Christ, Scripture exhorts us to "put to death the misdeeds of the body" that we may live (Ro 8:13). We hope Appendix B, starting on page 96, will shed light on this potentially confusing topic.

## What It Takes to Change

So much for the foundation for victory. How does it work out in actual practice?

I have had many opportunities to lean on these truths in my own life and pastoral ministry. On more than one occasion, men struggling with sexual fantasies have asked me for help in renewing their mind. Lust is a matter starkly antithetical to the whole notion of holiness. Those dealing with it are desperate for deliverance. But lasting help rarely comes immediately.

I recall one man in his early thirties who displayed the proper attitude toward this problem. His conscience had been awakened and he saw his sin in the light of God's holiness. Because he wanted to be free to glorify God he was very motivated and willing to do the work necessary to grow in holiness. These were the thoughts I shared with him from Romans 6:

**Know the truth.** *"For we know* that our old self was cru-cified with him so that the body of sin might be done away with, that we should no longer be slaves to sin" (Ro 6:6)

**For Further Study:**
Read Ephesians 4:22-24. What practical steps can you take to implement this command?

We must first *know* in order to believe. Spiritual knowledge precedes faith. I suggested to this man that he start by memorizing the sixth chapter of Romans. Paul later states that "the mind controlled by the Spirit is life and peace" (Ro 8:6). What better way to be spiritually minded than to fill one's mind with Scripture?

It is much easier to follow Jesus' example of fighting temptation with the Word of God when that Word has

Answers: F, F, F, T

33

been stored in the heart. "I have hidden your word in my heart that I may not sin against you" (Ps 119:11). We need to have the truth in our hearts and on the tips of our tongues. As we memorize and meditate on Scripture, we'll be transformed from spiritual pushovers who cave in to the slightest temptation to spiritual warriors who say, "We died to sin; how can we live in it any longer?"

**Count it to be true.** "The death he died, he died to sin once for all; but the life he lives, he lives to God. In the same way, *count yourselves dead to sin* but alive to God in Christ Jesus. (Ro 6:10-11, emphasis added)

"This is no game of 'let's pretend,'" writes theologian F.F. Bruce. "Believers should consider themselves to be what God in fact has made them."[11] Because we are dead to sin, the penalty and guilt of sin is no longer an issue. We have Jesus to thank for that. But beyond this, we are no longer obligated to sin, because sin is no longer our master. Its dominion is over. And not only have we died to sin, but we are alive to God in Christ Jesus! This phrase brings us back once again to our union with Christ and all the blessings associated with that happy principle.[12]

"Count yourselves dead" uses an accounting term which could also be translated "reckon" or "calculate." If I were trustworthy and told you I had deposited money in your bank account, you would count on it being there. In essence, Paul is saying, "Don't act like a loser, because you're not a loser. Act like the child of God you are."

**5** Battling sin begins in your mind. Draw a line connecting each of the destructive thoughts below with the verse that most effectively refutes it.

- "I'm all alone tonight... what if someone breaks in?"      **Php 4:13**

- "I'm so ugly and fat—there's no use sticking to this diet."      **1Co 10:13**

- "I just don't have the guts to tell my boss about Jesus."      **2Ti 1:7**

- "I'll never be able to maintain my virginity."      **Mt 19:26**

- "How could I possibly forgive him for what he did?"      **Ps 139:14**

**Offer yourself to God.** "Do not offer the parts of your body to sin, as instruments of wickedness, but rather *offer yourselves to God*, as those who have been brought from death to life; and offer the parts of your body to him as instruments of righteousness." (Ro 6:13, emphasis added)

We have a choice to make—many choices—every day.

We may offer the parts of our body to God for use in righteousness, or we may offer them for wicked use. Our minds, tongues, eyes, and other parts of our body are themselves morally neutral. But the way in which we choose to use them determines whether we honor or grieve God.

Sinful habits do not develop overnight, and rarely are they changed overnight. Only through the persistent application of God's truth can they be overcome. But as Jay Adams notes, this requires perseverance:

> Too many Christians give up. They want the change too soon. What they really want is change without the daily struggle. Sometimes they give up when they are on the very threshold of success. They stop before receiving. It usually takes at least three weeks of proper daily effort for one to feel comfortable in performing a new practice. And it takes about three more weeks to make the practice part of oneself. Yet, many Christians do not continue even for three days. If they do not receive instant success, they get discouraged. They want what they want now, and if they don't get it now, they quit.[14]

One lady I know had been plagued with fearful and depressing thoughts stemming from sins committed against her in years past. Her negative thoughts had her in a spiritual prison. If she reflected on those former experiences or encountered a present difficulty, a phonograph needle in her mind would come down and begin playing a familiar time-worn blues LP. Thought patterns repeated over the years had worn deep mental grooves which played the same depressing songs over and over again.

> 66 There are only these two ways of life: the feeling-motivated life of sin oriented toward self, and the commandment-oriented life of holiness oriented toward God. Living according to feeling rather than God's commandment is a fundamental hindrance to godliness...It is a clever 'wile' of Satan to tempt men to think that they cannot *do* what God requires because they do not *feel* like doing it, or that they must *do* what they feel like doing and cannot help themselves.[13] 99
>
> — **Jay Adams**

But then she learned she didn't have to sing along. Christ Jesus died on the cross to shatter those records. As that awareness grew, she began to recognize the old melancholic tunes when they began and quickly replaced them with new songs from God's Word.

When people hear the liberating truth that past experiences need no longer dictate their present actions, hope springs up in their hearts. It's no longer *our* past, but *Christ's* past that is now the decisive factor in our lives, because we're united with him in his death and his new life. I have had to learn that when memories of past sins crowd into my mind, I must refer immediately to my union with Jesus Christ. Now, rather than being paralyzed by condemnation, I'm typically able to turn such memories into an opportunity to thank God for forgiving my sin...even *that* one.

Lancaster, Pennsylvania is home to an excellent ministry for unwed mothers. The House of His Creation was founded and led by Jim and Anne Pierson for many years. On one occasion Anne told me of a recurring difficulty their young women faced. Many of these girls had become pregnant as a result of sexual sin, but came to believe in Jesus and receive his forgiveness. About five months into their pregnancies, however, when they began to feel their babies move within them, they would be reminded vividly of their former sins. Each new kick or internal somersault multiplied their guilt and discouragement.

But the Piersons beat the accuser at his own game. Anne taught the young women to let the baby's movement serve as a reminder that God had indeed forgiven them, and that he would cause all things to work together for their good. What a wise and creative way to deal with condemnation!

Through our union with Christ, we have died to the penalty and power of sin. His crucified body has atoned for our guilt, just as his resurrected body is our promise of victory. Our union with Christ is the basis for our deliverance from the bondage of sin. It is as immovable as it is unmerited; as sufficient as it is certain. If we will but seek to *know* the truth, *consider* it to be so, and then *offer* ourselves in consistent obedience to God, we will go from faith to faith, strength to strength, and glory to glory. ∎

> " Believe God's Word and power more than you believe your own feelings and experiences. Your Rock is Christ, and it is not the Rock which ebbs and flows, but your sea.[15] "
>
> — Samuel Rutherford

1. Have you ever identified so closely with someone else's experience that it felt you had experienced it yourself?

2. In your own words, try to describe this mystery of being united with Christ.

3. How can we reckon ourselves "dead to sin" when we are still so susceptible to temptation?

4. In light of this chapter, how would you explain 1 John 2:1?

5. "It's not that we're not *able* to sin," writes the author, "but that we're able *not* to sin." (Page 32) What does he mean?

6. How will this chapter change the way you resist sin?

**RECOMMENDED READING** *Men Made New* by John R.W. Stott (Grand Rapids, MI: Baker Book House, 1966, 1984)

*Romans Chapter Six: The New Man* by D. Martyn Lloyd-Jones (Grand Rapids, MI: Zondervan Publishing House, 1972)

CHAPTER FOUR

# THE BATTLE AGAINST SIN

C.J. MAHANEY

I n his book titled *A Nation Of Victims: The Decay Of The American Character*, author Charles Sykes makes the following observation: "Over the last half century, the triumph of therapeutic thinking has been so complete that it is frequently taken for granted; what began with Dr. Freud is now the staple of daytime television talk shows, routine in politics, almost reflexive in matters of criminal justice and ethics."[1]

Whether or not you've heard the phrase, you've no doubt encountered therapeutic thinking. It shows up in the courtroom when a serial killer's attorney asks for leniency on the grounds that his client was routinely abused by an alcoholic father. It claims most of us grew up in "dysfunctional" families, thus offering a ready-made explanation and excuse for our behavior. Rather than emphasizing personal responsibility, it stresses the way we've been psychologically affected by others or by our environment. As social scientist Dr. James Deese notes, therapeutic thinking "is so ingrained in modern American attitudes as hardly to be challenged."[2]

Surprisingly, the one institution best equipped to challenge the therapeutic trend has actually contributed to its popularity. I'm speaking of the Church. Rather than expose the errors of psychotherapy, the American Church in most cases has given uncritical acceptance...though there are some outspoken exceptions. In his book *Biblical Medical Ethics*, Dr. Franklin Payne comments, "Psychotherapy, as psychology and psychiatry, needs the most critical and detailed examination by evangelical Christians...Many Christians are influenced more by the concepts of secular psychotherapists than by the Word of God."[3]

I've met many of the Christians Dr. Payne is describing. Not long ago I was asked to speak at a men's retreat

**Meditate on Colossians 2:8.** How can we protect ourselves from being taken captive?

in another church. At the end of one session I was approached by a man who introduced himself and then began telling me about his difficult situation. He had grown up in a dysfunctional family. He was a codependent. He suffered from low self-esteem. In the space of the first two minutes he must have used almost every psychological buzz word in existence.

It was an awkward encounter. I wasn't eager to disagree with him or correct him. I had never met the man before, and I wanted him to experience my care and concern. But as he went on and on it seemed obvious he assumed I agreed with him. And I didn't. Why? Though he spoke psychobabble fluently, his diagnosis omitted any reference to the "S" word....

Sin.

**1** What things in Jesus' life might cause a counselor to recommend that he join the "recovery movement"?

Such omissions regrettably are the norm today in popular Christian literature and radio talk shows. We are pursuing a deeper understanding of ourselves (as defined by the recovery movement) rather than a deeper conviction of sin (as defined in Scripture). We have become more concerned about our own needs and feelings than about the character and commands of God. No wonder we aren't maturing as he intends.

## Our Most Serious Problem

Writing a century ago, J.C. Ryle offered a sharp but simple explanation for the deficiencies he observed in the Church: "Dim or indistinct views of sin are the origin of most of the errors, heresies and false doctrines of the present day...I believe that one of the chief wants of the church in the nineteenth century has been, and is, clearer, fuller teaching about sin."[5] If this was accurate during his generation, how much more so today.

But we've gone a step further. Contemporary teaching about self-esteem has replaced the doctrine of sin. Consider this remark from one well-known author:

> I don't think anything has been done in the name of Christ and under the banner of Christianity that has

> ❝ To say that our first need in life is to learn about sin may sound strange, but in the sense intended it is profoundly true. If you have not learned about sin, you cannot understand yourself, or your fellow-men, or the world you live in, or the Christian faith. And you will not be able to make head or tail of the Bible. For the Bible is an exposition of God's answer to the problem of human sin, and unless you have that problem clearly before you, you will keep missing the point of what it says...It is clear, therefore, that we need to fix in our minds what our ancestors would have called 'clear views of sin.'[6] ❞
>
> — J.I. Packer

proven more destructive to human personality, and hence counterproductive to the evangelistic enterprise, than the unchristian, uncouth strategy of attempting to make people aware of their lost and sinful condition.[7]

This pastor says that labeling sin as "rebellion against God" is "shallow and insulting to the human being."[8] His conviction about man's inherent worth leads him to the remarkable conclusion that a new "reformation" is in order. Where Martin Luther's emphasis on salvation by grace through faith transformed the Church in the sixteenth century, he argues, today's churches must recognize the sacred right of every person to self-esteem.

I do not question the man's sincerity, but his statements are bogus. They are, in fact, false doctrine. The modern emphasis on self-esteem has become an unacceptable alternative to the biblical doctrines of justification and sanctification.

*Justification.* Jesus did not die on the cross to improve our self-esteem. He died to atone for our sin. And yet the cross *does* teach us a crucial lesson about our worth: We are each worthy of the wrath of God. As a manifestation of God's unmerited mercy, the cross reveals the depth and seriousness of our sin. Anthony Hoekema points this out:

**For Further Study:**
The *NIV Complete Concordance* lists 466 occurrences of the word "sin" (or a derivative) in Scripture. For a biblical understanding of this vital subject...just start reading.

> In today's world there is little emphasis on the biblical doctrine of sin. But a person with a shallow sense of sin and of the wrath of God against our sin will neither feel the need for nor understand the biblical doctrine of justification. When sin is ignored, minimized or redefined we no longer live aware of our desperate need for Jesus Christ nor appreciative of what he accomplished on the cross for us.[10]

Unless we understand the nature of sin and how offensive

it is to God, we'll never understand why the cross was necessary. We'll never be amazed by grace.

*Sanctification.* A clear understanding of the doctrine of sin is imperative for sanctification as well. Scripture reveals that our most serious hindrance to growth is sin against God. The recovery movement, on the other hand, insists that unmet needs, pain, damaged emotions, or low self-esteem are the root of our difficulties. The two conclusions are irreconcilably opposed.

I am not denying the reality or severity of the pain we experience when others sin against us. It is critical I not be misunderstood here. The Bible makes numerous references to those who are afflicted and oppressed. But please understand: *Pain is not our root problem.* Jesus said, "For from *within,* out of men's hearts, come evil thoughts, sexual immorality, theft, murder, adultery, greed, malice, deceit, lewdness, envy, slander, arrogance, and folly. All these evils come from *inside* and make a man 'unclean'" (Mk 7:21-23, emphasis added; see also Jas 1:14-15).

**For Further Study:**
Many of the Bible's references to God's compassion can be found in the Psalms (9:12,18; 34:18; 147:3) and Isaiah (49:13; 61:1).

Too many of us "feel the reality of our wounds more than the fact of our sin."[11] But if we genuinely want to be conformed to the image of Jesus Christ, this will have to change. Our freedom and maturity depend on it. The therapeutic model misdiagnoses our root problem, and thus proves incapable of providing an effective solution. But once we recognize sin as the source of our problem, suddenly we have a scriptural solution and biblical hope for change. It's called the doctrine of sanctification.

## Mowing Your Own Lawn

Sanctification is a lifelong process of repentance (not recovery) and obedience (not inner healing) that results in holiness (not wholeness) for the glory of God (not personal fulfillment). This doctrine is succinctly stated in Colossians 3:1-17. If you haven't already done so, please take a minute to read that passage before you continue.

**Meditate on Colossians 1:15-20.** Judging by this description, do you think Jesus is sufficient to regenerate and redeem you?

It's important to see the transition Paul is making in this third chapter. The first two chapters of Colossians emphasize the supremacy and sufficiency of Christ. He stresses this again at the beginning of Chapter 3. Paul consciously refrained from teaching the Colossians about sanctification until they had first understood Christ's work for them and within them. Until they grasped what it meant to be reconciled to and regenerated by God, he knew they would not be properly motivated by grace.

Neither will we. This is why the second and third chapters of this book highlight regeneration and our union with Christ. We have also written a book on the doctrine of justification called *This Great Salvation.* Like Paul, we want to motivate by grace. Once that foundation is established, then we can pursue godliness without straying toward legalism or license.

Paul defines the process of sanctification with two striking phrases: We are to "rid ourselves" of sin and "clothe ourselves" with righteousness (Col 3:8,12). It is only because of what Christ has accomplished on the cross and the miracle of regeneration that we are able to obey these commands. And yet those two supernatural imperatives now leave us without excuse. If grace does not result in godliness, then we have not accurately understood grace. God fully expects us to change, grow, and mature. As F.F. Bruce exhorts, "Now be (in actual practice) what you now are (by a divine act)."[12]

Please note that Paul says we are to "rid *ourselves*" and "clothe *ourselves*." We have the privilege and responsibility of participating in change. Though sanctification is no less a supernatural work of the Holy Spirit than regeneration, there is one fundamental difference: in sanctification we have a critical role to

> ❝ Though the power for godly character comes from Christ, the responsibility for developing and displaying that character is ours. This principle seems to be one of the most difficult for us to understand and apply. One day we sense our personal responsibility and seek to live a godly life by the strength of our own will power. The next day, realizing the futility of trusting in ourselves, we turn it all over to Christ and abdicate our responsibility which is set forth in the Scriptures. We need to learn that the Bible teaches both total responsibility and total dependence in all aspects of the Christian life.[13] ❞
>
> — Jerry Bridges

play. "God works in us and with us," said the great Puritan pastor John Owen, "not against us or without us."

Statements such as "Stop trying and start trusting" or "Let go and let God" make popular plaques but poor theology. Those who claim "All effort is wrong" are badly mistaken. Actually, the Bible instructs us to "Make *every* effort...to be holy; without holiness no one will see the Lord" (Heb 12:14, emphasis added). This is grace-motivated effort, of course, but it's effort nonetheless. God hasn't told us to pray or simply trust him for godliness; he says "train *yourself* to be godly" (1Ti 4:7, emphasis added). We are to obey in the power of the Holy Spirit.

Paul clarifies this combination of God's work and our responsibility when he writes, "Continue to work out (not work *for*) your salvation with fear and trembling, for it is God who works in you to will and to act according to his good purpose" (Php 2:12-13). Though our effort apart from God's work would be futile, sanctification cannot be delegated to God. Each of us must mow his own lawn.

What form does our responsibility take? How do we fulfill the biblical command to rid ourselves of sin? Scripture offers a two-part strategy.

**For Further Study:**
How would you answer someone who concluded that "all effort is wrong" after reading Zechariah 4:6?

## Strategy #1: Attack Sin

I love the offensive posture of the New Testament toward sin. Nowhere is that more evident than in the Apostle Paul's terse command to the Colossians: "Put to death, therefore, whatever belongs to your earthly nature" (Col 3:5). In the battle for personal holiness, aggressiveness is both a command and a necessity. We must be ruthless. We must go on the attack.

Paul uses a violent metaphor here not simply to get our attention but to underscore a critical aspect of sanctification. We are to kill any and all manifestations of sin in our hearts. We must take the initiative to execute sin daily.

> **"** We need to cultivate in our own hearts the same hatred of sin God has. Hatred of sin as sin, not just as something disquieting or defeating to ourselves, but as displeasing to God, lies at the root of all holiness.[14] **"**
>
> — **Jerry Bridges**

Jesus went so far as to say, "If your right eye causes you to sin, gouge it out and throw it away. It is better for you to lose one part of your body than for your whole body to be thrown into hell" (Mt 5:29). He also recommended amputating a hand for the

44

same reason. Was Jesus commanding actual surgery here? I think not, because a hand or eye isn't the root cause. Jesus purposely used vivid imagery to make a point: We must recognize the seriousness of sin and deal decisively with it. Resisting sin when tempted is not sufficient. We must take drastic steps to attack and kill sin in our lives. John Owen exhorts us to pursue "a victory over it, and pursuit of it to a complete conquest...sin will not otherwise die, but by being gradually and constantly weakened; spare it, and it heals its wounds, and recovers strength."[15]

The spiritual discipline of putting sin to death, otherwise known as mortification, is a neglected area of truth. Most of us are about as familiar with this subject as we are with outhouses. "Our forefathers used to speak of mortifying sin," notes Sinclair Ferguson.[16] And J.I. Packer laments, "It is a theme on which no contemporary writing of significance seems to be available."[17] That's not surprising, but it is revealing. Can you imagine a book titled *Put Sin To Death!* as a Christian bestseller?

Mortification is not popular because it tends to be difficult. Ask the person trying to submit cheerfully to a boss who has repeatedly denied a promotion. Ask the recently converted, unmarried couple who must now control sexual urges they have gratified for years. But listen: this is not weekend golf we're playing here. This is war. Holiness and discipleship are war.

Attacking sin isn't complex. And though I want to say this sensitively, I also want to say it firmly: Your ability to attack sin doesn't depend on your past. We have no acceptable excuse for sinning. It's never to be viewed as an understandable weakness.

Living as a Christian means living in the trenches. Sinclair Ferguson says it as well as anyone could:

> What then is this killing of sin? It is the constant battle against sin which we fight daily—the refusal to allow the eye to wander, the mind to contemplate, the affec-

**Meditate on 2 Corinthians 10:3-5.**
In terms of spiritual warfare, was Paul a "hawk" or a "dove"?

❝ We may take comfort about our souls if we know anything of an inward fight and conflict. It is the invariable companion of genuine Christian holiness...Do we find in our heart of hearts a spiritual struggle? Do we feel anything of the flesh lusting against the spirit and the spirit against the flesh...? Are we conscious of two principles within us, contending for the mastery? Do we feel anything of war in our inward man? Well, let us thank God for it! It is a good sign. It is strongly probable evidence of the great work of sanctification...We are evidently no friends of Satan...The very fact that he assaults us should fill our minds with hope.[18] ❞

— J.C. Ryle

tions to run after anything which will draw us from Christ. It is the deliberate rejection of any sinful thought, suggestion, desire, aspiration, deed, circumstance or provocation at the moment we become conscious of its existence. It is the consistent endeavor to do all in our powers to weaken the grip which sin in general, and its manifestations in our own lives in particular, has. It is not accomplished only by saying 'no' to what is wrong, but by a determined acceptance of all the good and spiritually nourishing disciplines of the gospel.[19]

**Meditate on Galatians 5:16-17.** Why does every genuine Christian experience inner turmoil?

Does this describe your attitude? Toward which end are your energies primarily directed, recreation or righteousness? Self-indulgence or self-control? Are you prepared to do whatever it takes to win the war? If so, what is your strategy for attacking the sin in your life right now?

## Strategy #2: Avoid Sin

Attacking sin is not all that's involved in the sanctification process. We must avoid sin as well. As followers of Jesus Christ, we are called to a lifestyle that is distinct from our surrounding culture: "Since we have these promises, dear friends, let us purify ourselves from everything that contaminates body and spirit, perfecting holiness out of reverence for God" (2Co 7:1). What are these promises that motivate us to purify ourselves and pursue holiness? God's own offer to be uniquely present among his people as we separate ourselves from the world: "'I will live with them and walk among them, and I will be their God, and they will be my people'" (2Co 6:16).

**For Further Study:** Read James 1:27. Can you list two or three specific ways in which a Christian might be "polluted by the world"?

In a sense it would be easier if God told us to separate ourselves *physically* from the culture. Yet God specifically forbids that (1Co 5:9-10), and instead appoints us as ambassadors (2Co 5:18-20). No ambassador works effectively in isolation. We are to relate to our culture without *reflecting* our culture, always navigating between the secular and the self-righteous.

Our flesh constantly begs to be indulged, yet Paul tells us to "make no provision for the flesh in regard to its lusts" (Ro 13:14 NAS). That means distancing ourselves from anything that's likely to tempt us to sin. Paul told the Corinthians the same thing in even clearer terms: "Flee immorality" (1Co 6:18 NAS)...don't fight with it.

Though Joseph lived long before the New Testament was written, he exemplifies the way we should avoid sin

**2** When temptation hits, we have two basic responses: fight or flight. Check what you think would be the appropriate response to each of the temptations listed below:

| Scenario | Fight | Flight |
|---|---|---|
| Sudden fear that someone will rob your home | ❏ | ❏ |
| Curiosity about *Playboy's* issue on Middle East politics | ❏ | ❏ |
| Urge to "go into hibernation" when friends let you down | ❏ | ❏ |
| Strong sense of anger when child spills your coffee | ❏ | ❏ |
| Desire to swing by the bar "just to see old friends" | ❏ | ❏ |

(Ge 39:6-20). For some time his master's wife had sought to seduce him. Finally, frustrated by his integrity, she grabbed him by the cloak and said, "Come to bed with me!"

Now Joseph *could* have viewed this as a divine appointment. He could have thought, "This may be the ideal opportunity for me to share with her what God has done in my life." But he didn't flirt with the temptation. He didn't even fight it. He simply fled, leaving Potiphar's wife holding his cloak.

I can imagine one of the servants walking outside the house when suddenly, whoosh! A human-shaped blur flashes out the door at world-class speed.

"What was that?"

Joseph. The man of God. Running for his life.

"Lord!" he pants at the half-mile mark, "help me!"

"I am. Just keep running. You get away from that woman as far and as fast as you can."

It's smart to run from temptation. It's idiotic to stand there and try to stare it down. And yet some would have responded to Joseph's situation this way:

"God, I sense temptation beginning to develop. I call upon you, Lord. Please deliver me from this situation."

> **❝** To labor to be acquainted with the ways, wiles, methods, advantages, and occasions of the success of sin is the beginning to this warfare.[20] **❞**
> — **John Owen**

"I *am* going to deliver you," God says. "Run!"

"Lord, I'm trusting you for deliverance. Deliver me right now from this feeling of lust."

"That won't happen till I return, and I'm not coming back in the next five minutes. Hit the road, Mr. Potato Head!"

"Lord, I thank you. You've caused me to be born again, and I know your power is at work in me. Greater is he who is in me than he who is in the world."

"Yes, that's right, and the Greater One is saying, 'Move!' Move your body and move it now!"

If you're serious about sanctification, you're not trying

**Meditate on
1 Timothy 6:11.** How
long does it take you,
on average, to flee from
temptation once you've
recognized it?

to see how close you can get to the curb. You're prepared
to drive on the other side of the street, if necessary, to
avoid sin. And in areas where you know you're vulnerable,
you're obeying the command of Jesus: "Watch and pray so
that you will not fall into temptation" (Mt 26:41).

We need to cultivate the ability to discern where we are
most prone to sin. That way we'll be able to develop a
strategy for avoiding temptation. Areas of vulnerability
will differ, but watching isn't optional for any of us.

In what area(s) do you need to develop a strategy of
avoidance? You can probably begin with whatever you've
been thinking about as you read this section.

## A New Set of Clothes

As we saw earlier in Colossians, ridding ourselves of sin
is just half of the equation. Paul exhorts us, "Therefore, as
God's chosen people, holy and dearly loved, *clothe yourselves*
with compassion, kindness, humility, gentleness and
patience" (Col 3:12, emphasis added). Not only must we
put off sin, but we must put on righteousness (Eph 4:22-24).

"These two factors," writes Jay Adams, "always must be
present in order to effect genuine change. Putting off will
not be permanent without putting on. Putting on is hypo-
critical as well as temporary, unless it is accompanied by
putting off...Sanctification continues as the believer daily
turns *from* sin / *to* righteousness."[21]

**For Further Study:**
Read Revelation 3:4-6.
Can you identify four
promises in this
passage?

For example, if God has exposed materialism or greed
in your heart, repent and then begin systematically to
replace it with generosity. Start with faithfulness in
tithing to your local church; add to that offerings, and
look for opportunities to give secretly as well. Perhaps you
tend to criticize others. If so, confess the sin of pride and
consciously focus on encouraging and honoring others
instead. If selfishness is a recurring theme, place yourself
in situations where you are required to serve.

What should immediately be obvious is that character
cannot be developed or refined in isolation. To cultivate a
righteous and fruitful life we need the context of a local
church. For example, I may be the model of patience...as
long as I'm alone. I could spend days studying the subject
of compassion without ever encountering someone who
needed care. Unless I interact with others I'm simply incapable of assessing where I need to grow.

The fact is, there are very few Christ-like traits we can
develop apart from relationships in the church. We need

people to practice on! If we're intent on change, we'll commit ourselves to a church where individuals take seriously the biblical exhortations to encourage and correct.

As you've probably perceived by now, battling sin does not happen effortlessly. It involves genuine confession, repentance, obedience to Scripture, accountability to oth-

---

**3** After reading Colossians 3:12-17, select the Christian character trait mentioned there (humility, forbearance, etc.) that you would most like to develop. In the next week or two, set aside as many as five devotional times to meditate on Scriptures highlighting this area. Also, ask God for specific ways to apply what you learn.

**Character Trait:** _____

**Day One:**

Scripture(s)            Insights            Application

**Day Two:**

Scripture(s)            Insights            Application

**Day Three:**

Scripture(s)            Insights            Application

**Day Four:**

Scripture(s)            Insights            Application

**Day Five:**

Scripture(s)            Insights            Application

ers, and the consistent practice of the spiritual disciplines. You'll also need courage and perseverance. "There are no quick and easy paths to spiritual maturity," says R.C. Sproul. "The soul that seeks a deeper level of maturity must be prepared for a long, arduous task."[22]

But do you know what it feels like to grow? To sense God's pleasure and presence? To hear his voice? To know you are contributing to the advancement of his kingdom? Nothing compares with that experience. And this is God's amazing reward for all those willing to put off sin and put on righteousness.

Let me impart fresh hope to you. No matter what you have experienced in the past, you—by the grace of God—*can* change. Through a determined strategy to attack and avoid sin and clothe yourself with righteousness, you can be a dramatically different person at this time next year. ■

**GROUP DISCUSSION**

1. Imagine you are on the jury trying the serial killer mentioned on page 39. It's clear the man was frequently beaten by his alcoholic father during childhood. How much of a factor would that be in reaching your verdict?

2. "We have become more concerned about our own needs and feelings than about the character and commands of God," says the author. (Page 40) What's an example?

3. What does "self-esteem" mean to you?

4. Does the message of the cross make you more or less secure about your identity?

5. Why is the recovery movement incapable of meeting our deepest needs?

6. Identify the root problem in each of the following scenarios:

—Since being raped in college, Ann has strongly disliked and distrusted men

—Bill is seeking a divorce because his wife shows him little affection

—When under intense pressure, Mary entertains thoughts of suicide

—Rob, who grew up visiting his father only on weekends, is a workaholic

7. What's the biggest distinction between sanctification and regeneration?

8. Why are relationships in the church so essential for character growth?

9. In what area of your life do you most need a "new set of clothes"?

**RECOMMENDED READING**

*The Pursuit of Holiness* by Jerry Bridges (Colorado Springs, CO: NavPress, 1978)

*The Practice of Godliness* by Jerry Bridges (Colorado Springs, CO: NavPress, 1983)

*Holiness* by J.C. Ryle (Welwyn, Hertfordshire, England: Evangelical Press, 1979)

*The Enemy Within* by Kris Lundgaard (Phillipsburg, NJ: P&R Publishing, 1998)

# CHAPTER FIVE

# TOOLS OF THE TRADE (I)

ROBIN BOISVERT

B ack in the days when a pack of cigarettes still cost 35 cents, I was a heavy smoker. Some might say a nicotine fiend, a Chesterfield-regular kind of guy. I was addicted to smoking and I knew it.

Quitting was no problem—I had quit a dozen times. But when the urge to smoke became too strong, I would start back up again. So I decided to stop buying cigarettes. That didn't work either. It only made me a nuisance to my friends since I was always bumming smokes from them. At my lowest point, I was scavenging half-smoked butts out of the ash tray.

Around this time I became aware the Holy Spirit was convicting me of sin and drawing me toward Jesus. Though my smoking was just one evidence of my internal state, it seemed symbolic of my whole life. I was stuck. Every attempt to stop smoking had failed. I could not see how I would ever be able to overcome this habit. I wasn't even sure I wanted to.

I knew Jesus was primarily after my heart, not my habit. Still, I couldn't imagine following him and smoking at the same time. So one evening I asked Larry, a believer I had just met, if a guy could be a Christian and still smoke. This was my version of the trick question the Pharisees asked Jesus about paying taxes to Caesar. They thought they could trap him no matter which way he answered.

My strategy went like this. If Larry replied, "No—one cannot be a Christian and smoke," I would solemnly pronounce his answer to be legalistic and contrary to the principle that God looks at the heart. On the other hand, if he said, "Yes, no problem," then I could dismiss Christianity as a meaningless set of powerless beliefs. Yet the question wasn't entirely cynical. Part of me desperately wanted to believe—and be free.

Well, Larry gave me an answer I hadn't counted on.

**Meditate on Romans 8:29.** What is one aspect of Jesus' character you would really like to see in your own life?

"Suppose," he said, "you wanted to encourage someone to trust in the Lord. Do you think you'd be more effective as a witness *with* a cigarette in your hand or *without* one?"

Hmmmm…good response. Suddenly the issue wasn't smoking, but whether or not I wanted my life to glorify God. It was really a question of motive.

I'm now of the opinion that no person with true faith in Jesus Christ will be barred from heaven for having a pack of cigarettes in his pocket. But that's beside the point, for God's goal in sanctification is that we be conformed to the image of Jesus Christ. And I can't picture Jesus walking up to the woman at the well (Jn 4:7-18) and saying, "Got a light? Thanks. Now, let's talk about your sin. How many husbands have you got?"

By the way, I'm not a Chesterfield-regular kind of guy anymore. God had means available to help me kick the habit—the same means we'll be examining in these next two chapters. Of prior importance, though, was my motive. God will always help someone whose motive is right, who really wants to glorify him and do his will. But he will not let us use him merely to improve the quality of our lives or change our circumstances. He's after nothing less than our hearts. In holiness, motive always precedes means.

> **❝** Grace is not simply leniency when we have sinned. Grace is the enabling gift of God not to sin. Grace is power, not just pardon.[1] **❞**
>
> — **John Piper**

Before delving into the next section, let's quickly review what we've learned thus far about God's plan of sanctification. We are new creations who enjoy a living union with Jesus Christ. But we are still in a battle. We experience inward warfare and inward peace; we wrestle with sin and rest in Christ.

A clear understanding of this tension between the "now and the not yet" will guard you from some serious misconceptions. For example, just because you encounter severe temptations and spiritual battles doesn't necessarily mean you have done something wrong. A holy person is *not* one who never has any spiritual conflicts, or has achieved perfection. Rather, a holy person is one who is becoming more Christlike through the process of obeying God amidst life's daily struggles.

**1** Can you locate one Bible verse that shows we are powerless to earn God's salvation? Write it out in the space below. (If you're stumped, try Ephesians, Chapter 2.)

## Learning from a Master

Like most men, I have a fondness for tools. I can still recall my excitement when my friends gave me a brand-new, fully equipped toolbox at my bachelor's party. I could hardly wait for the party to end so I could play with my new tools. In fact, I was so eager that I gashed my finger trying to get the toolbox open.

Any genuine Christian will admit that he or she is in serious need of spiritual repair. What assurance we have in knowing the Holy Spirit has the right tools to make those repairs—to sanctify us! More importantly, he is personally responsible for teaching us how to use those tools so that we mature and change. And he can show us how to use them without hurting ourselves.

As the third person of the Godhead, the Holy Spirit is the One who effects change in our lives. But he's not merely a specialist in sanctification. God's Spirit is involved in our salvation from start to finish. To be regenerated (born again) is to be born of the Spirit. Both repentance and faith—the two sides of conversion—are gifts the Spirit gives.[2] He is active in our justification and adoption. He fills us, intercedes for us, seals us in Christ for the day of redemption, and will ultimately glorify us.

**For Further Study:**
Read Romans 3:9-12. Do you consider this a fair description of yourself? If not, what biblical evidence do you find to the contrary?

> ❝ God does not leave even the issue of conversion finally in the hands of man...Nor does God leave to uncertain risk our growth and perseverance and holiness. Rather, he says, 'I will put my Spirit within you, and will cause you to walk in my statutes and be careful to observe my ordinances' (Ezekiel 36:27). It is the Lord himself who works in us to will and to do his good pleasure (Philippians 2:12-13; Hebrews 13:21).[3] ❞
>
> — John Piper

But we are concerned now with the Holy Spirit in his sanctifying role. We are those "who have been chosen according to the foreknowledge of God the Father, *through the sanctifying work of the Spirit*, for obedience to Jesus Christ and sprinkling by his blood" (1Pe 1:2, emphasis added). Throughout the rest of this chapter and the next, we will examine some of the tools with which he so effectively works in us.

## The Word of God

The Bible is God's unique revelation to man. It tells us truths we could never find in any other source, such as how the world began, what happens after we die, and so on. It also tells us some things we would never have *want-*

*ed* to find out: we are born in sin, we're in need of redemption, and we are unable to please God by ourselves. Someone has remarked that the Bible must be the Word of God because man would never write anything so disapproving of himself!

The Bible does not flatter us, nor does it teach—as virtually every other religion does—that man can perfect himself. In fact, Scripture is pessimistic in the extreme regarding man's innate ability. That's why it is such a valuable and essential tool in man's sanctification. Jesus himself confirmed this in praying to his Father, "Sanctify them by the truth; your word is truth" (Jn 17:17).

John Bunyan's classic *Pilgrim's Progress* begins with the hero, Christian, finding "the book"…and that was the start of his troubles. But it was also the beginning of the end of his troubles. The Holy Spirit and the Bible conspire together to *convict* us of our great need for God. Yet as Christian discovered, they convict us in order to *convert* us, and they convert us in order to *transform* us:

> But as for you, continue in what you have learned and have become convinced of, because you know those from whom you learned it, and how from infancy you have known the holy Scriptures, which are able to make you wise for salvation through faith in Christ Jesus. All Scripture is God-breathed and is useful for teaching, rebuking, correcting and training in righteousness. (2Ti 3:14-16)

As Paul makes clear in this letter to Timothy, Scripture has a unique power to produce change in the Christian. It *teaches* us God's laws and ways, then *reproves* us when we fall short of that instruction. But it *corrects* us as well. It doesn't just tell us we're wrong; it lifts us back up and sets us on the right path. Finally, it *trains us in righteousness*, showing us how to live.

Have you ever noticed how many vivid metaphors are used to describe the Word of God?

*It's our spiritual food and drink.* "Man does not live on bread alone but on every word that comes from the mouth of the Lord" (Dt 8:3). Scripture is both milk for the young and solid food for the mature (Heb 5:12-14).

*It's a mirror.* "Anyone who listens to the word but does not do what it says is like a man who looks at his face in a mirror and, after looking at himself, goes away and immediately forgets what he looks like" (Jas 1: 23-24). The Bible shows us ourselves as God sees us. It's a reality check, revealing who and what we really are.

**Meditate on Jeremiah 23:29.** Have you ever felt the power of God's Word as described in this passage?

**Meditate on Psalm 32:8-9.** If we ignore Scripture, God may have to pull out the bit and bridle.

56

*It's a light.* "Your word is a lamp to my feet and a light for my path" (Ps 119:105). Scripture shows us the way we should live and what we should avoid.

*It's seed.* "The farmer went out to sow...The seed is the word of God" (Lk 8:5,11). When planted in the good soil of a receptive heart, it bears much fruit.

*It's a sword.* "For the word of God is living and active. Sharper than any double-edged sword, it penetrates even to dividing soul and spirit, joints and marrow; it judges the thoughts and attitudes of the heart" (Heb 4:12).

What all these figures of speech have in common (and there are more) is the absolute necessity and usefulness of Scripture. Nothing about the Bible is superfluous, and it needs no supplement. It is sufficient for all things having to do with salvation and godliness, "so that the man of God may be thoroughly equipped for *every* good work" (2Ti 3:17).

In past generations, the inspiration and inerrancy of Holy Scripture has been repeatedly attacked. Today the Bible's sufficiency is questioned by those who suggest, both outright and subtly, that it is incapable of addressing some of humanity's deepest questions and fundamental needs. But the Bible is in no way dependent upon any outside source of knowledge. It is more than enough. This wonderful Book is the Holy Spirit's primary tool for changing us.

How does that change take place? By our hearing and applying the Word of God, otherwise known as obedience. That will only happen consistently as we commit to the following disciplines:

*Set aside a regular time to read the Bible...and make sure you keep the appointment.* First thing in the morning is for many the most effective time. Of course, that may mean going to bed earlier to insure you get enough sleep. If you aren't reading your Bible regularly, and you can't seem to fit it in, it's because something less important has become too important. Find out what it is and make changes. Be ruthless.

**For Further Study:** Is merely hearing the Word sufficient to produce change? (See Matthew 7:24-27; John 14:21-24; James 1:22)

> ❝ Some friends of mine practice a 'no Bible, no breakfast' discipline. Some read at night. Some spend time with God at other opportune times during the day. But I know of *no one* who has a deep spiritual walk who does not spend time daily with God in his Word. It is indispensable. It requires a specific commitment.[4] ❞
>
> **— Jerry White**

One major distraction is news and information. In this age of instant and global communication, many Christians

**2** According to a Barna survey, 73% of Americans say it is important to read the Bible. An amazing 93% of U.S. households have at least one Bible. But notice how often those Bibles actually get opened...then check the box that most accurately reflects your own reading habit.

In an average week, Americans read the Bible...

☐ Every day     12%

☐ Several days     15%

☐ One day     16%

☐ Never     57%

spend more time with newspapers, news magazines, and news broadcasts than they do with the Lord. There are now more things than ever to shock us, outrage us, frighten us, and usurp our precious time. But there is no possible way we can monitor or respond to all that is happening. Of course, I'm not suggesting ignorance or inaction, but if the daily paper or evening news crowds out your study of the Bible, then it's time to make major adjustments.

*Commit yourself to a specific plan of study.* Reading through the *NIV Study Bible* has worked well for me. This way I'm forced to read those portions of Scripture I might consider to be less important or less interesting. It takes a full reading of the Bible to develop a complete picture of God. As the late A.W. Tozer once said, "We can hold a correct view of truth only by daring to believe *everything* God has said about himself" (emphasis added).[5]

There are a number of good resources that can enhance your daily time in the Word. We've listed a few in the "Recommended Reading" section at the end of this chapter. Varying your approach from time to time will make this discipline more enjoyable and profitable.

*Find someone who will help you.* Your study of the Bible will be greatly accelerated as you interact with a Christian mentor. You'll learn lots simply by asking, "How do you study Scripture?" You'll also benefit (though not without some squirming) when he or she asks,

**For Further Study:**
Timothy benefited immensely from having Paul as his mentor. To glimpse the impact of this relationship read 2 Timothy 1:13-14 and 3:10-15.

❝ The word hidden conveys the thought of storing something up against a time of future need. We do this by meditating continually on God's Word, by constantly thinking about it, and applying its truths to the everyday situations of life. I personally have found a systematic Scripture memorization program to be absolutely necessary to continual meditation on God's Word. I cannot think throughout the day about what I do not have in my heart.[6] ❞

— **Jerry Bridges**

"So...are you actually doing it?" Accountability is a great asset. Just make sure the person holding you accountable doesn't have similar shortcomings—or the gift of mercy.

*Hide God's Word in your heart by memorizing Scripture.* Paul points out the inner transformation that occurs as we begin letting the Bible shape our thoughts and attitudes: "Do not conform any longer to the pattern of this world, but be transformed by the renewing of your mind. Then you will be able to test and approve what God's will is—his good, pleasing and perfect will" (Ro 12:2). Memorization may not come easily, but as you weave the Word into the fabric of your life, you'll be well prepared when temptation or adversity strikes.

## A Clear Conscience

> Here I stand. I cannot do otherwise…my conscience is captive to the Word of God. I cannot and will not recant anything, for to go against conscience is neither right nor safe. God help me. Amen.[7]

Luther's famous defense before the Diet of Worms (that was the name of the official council that tried him, I kid you not!) indicates what an important place conscience occupies in the life of the Christian. It also plays a major role in our sanctification.

Each of us has undoubtedly encountered this mysterious faculty called conscience. When, as a sixth-grader, I shot a rubber band into a group of students by the schoolroom door, I didn't expect it to hit anyone in the eye. But it did. And when my classmate screamed out in pain, neither she nor any of the others knew what had happened. My conscience knew, however, and insisted that I take responsibility for what I had done. I fought against it, trying every possible excuse, but to no avail. My conscience refused to let me off the hook. The only way to silence it was to admit my guilt and face the consequences.

This incident illustrates the most remarkable feature of conscience—the judgments it renders are completely objective and unbiased.[8] In other words, you can never win an argument with your conscience. It's always on the job, even in dreams. It can act as *witness*, telling what it sees or hears. It can act as *attorney*, prosecuting us for misdeeds or, on rare occasions, defending us. It may also act as *judge*, issuing categorical verdicts which cannot be appealed.

"You lied," proclaims conscience.

**Meditate on Romans 1:20-21.** Why is there no excuse for rejecting the moral law of God?

"I did not! I was just stating the truth in a certain way so as not to cause any unnecessary conflict."

"You lied."

Conscience doesn't argue the point. It just states it. This is why conscience drives some people to distraction and why they will go to great lengths to stifle it, or deaden it with alcohol and drugs.

> **" "** Great indeed is the power of con-
> science! Mighty is the influence which it is
> able to exercise on the hearts of men! It
> can strike terror into the minds of monarchs
> on their thrones. It can make multitudes
> tremble and shake before a few bold
> friends of truth like a flock of sheep. Blind
> and mistaken as conscience often is,
> unable to convert a man or lead him to
> Christ, it is still a most blessed part of
> man's constitution, and the best friend in
> the congregation that the preacher of the
> gospel has.[9]  **" "**
>
> — **J.C. Ryle**

The word itself means "to know together with." Theologian Ole Hallesby explains the significance of this definition:

> It is, then, not merely a knowing, a con-sciousness, but a *knowing together* with something or some-one. Nor need we be in doubt as to what it is that man in his con-science knows togeth-er with. Among all races…it is a charac-teristic of man that he in his conscience knows together with a will that is over and above his own…This will, which is the will of God, is what men call the law or the moral law, that is, the law according to which man's life should be lived.[10]

Though unbiased, conscience is not infallible. It may be misinformed. It may be overly sensitive. Or, if it has been routinely repressed, it may no longer be sensitive at all. A person who ignores his conscience is headed for dis-aster. He will soon lose the ability to distinguish right from wrong, good from evil. This explains a lot about our society…and about my initial exposure to drugs.

When I was eighteen years old a friend gave me a joint of marijuana. It was 1968 and drugs had just started to fil-ter into the suburbs of Washington, D.C. where I lived. I knew it was illegal. I knew it was wrong. My conscience was screaming at me…but I did it anyway. A couple of days later I smoked another joint, and again the siren of my conscience went off. Only this time it wasn't quite so loud. After a half dozen times, I could hardly hear it at all. As a result, I gradually lost my moral compass. On those rare occasions when I could faintly detect the voice of conscience, I regarded it as a nuisance and a killjoy.

If a man sears his conscience he will soon come to view it as a curse. But God endowed us with conscience in order to bless us. It's not always the bearer of unpleasant news. It can excuse as well as accuse, congratulate as well as condemn. And as Paul told young Timothy, conscience is an essential safeguard of the Christian life:

Timothy my son, I give you the following charge. And may I say before I give it to you, that it is in full accord with those prophecies made at your ordination, which sent you out to battle for the right armed only with your faith and a clear conscience. Some, alas, have laid these simple weapons contemptuously aside and, as far as their faith is concerned, have run their ships on the rocks. (1Ti 1:18-19 Phillips)

Conscience may be a simple weapon, but it is highly effective in the battle against sin. To lay it "contemptuously aside" is akin to spiritual suicide.

A clear conscience is one of the most precious benefits of the new birth. "Since we have confidence to enter the Most Holy Place by the blood of Jesus," says the writer of the book of Hebrews, "let us draw near to God with a sincere heart in full assurance of faith, having our hearts sprinkled to cleanse us from a guilty conscience" (Heb 10:19,22; cf. Heb 9:14). How gracious of Christ to scour away the foul stains of our past sins with his blood!

**3** Read Ephesians 4:25-32, then take a minute to listen to your conscience. Are you aware of any unconfessed offense against God or man?

Now that we have a clean conscience, we must put forth the effort to keep it that way.

Conscience acts as a warning light on the dashboard of our lives, and we need to heed its flashing. The procedure is the same as any auto mechanic would follow: determine the source of the difficulty and then set about to correct it. Usually the solution involves confessing sin and asking forgiveness.

After committing adultery with Bathsheba and murdering Uriah, King David chugged along for months ignoring the red light of his conscience. He recounts his experience for us in Psalm 32:

**Meditate on Acts 24:16.** Did Paul take conscience for granted?

Blessed is he whose transgressions are forgiven, whose sins are covered. Blessed is the man whose sin the Lord does not count against him and in whose spirit is no deceit. When I kept silent, my bones wasted away through my groaning all day long. For day and night your hand was heavy upon me; my strength was sapped as in the heat of summer. Then I acknowledged my sin to you and did not cover up my iniquity. I said, "I will confess my transgressions to the Lord"—and you forgave the guilt of my sin.

**For Further Study:**
Write Psalm 139:23-24 on an index card and put it in a place where it will serve as a daily reminder.

Therefore let everyone who is godly pray to you while you may be found; surely when the mighty waters rise, they will not reach him. (Ps 32:1-6)

As long as David was silent, his conscience wasn't. Unconfessed sin led to spiritual and physical affliction. But as soon as he acknowledged his deeds and repented, forgiveness and deliverance came. David's testimony shows that a clear conscience could cure a lot of the problems we have, including many labeled "mental illness" or "depression."

> 44 It is time for us Christians to face up to our responsibility for holiness. Too often we say we are 'defeated' by this or that sin. No, we are not defeated; we are simply disobedient. It might be well if we stopped using the terms 'victory' and 'defeat' to describe our progress in holiness. Rather we should use the terms 'obedience' and 'disobedience.'[11] 77
>
> — **Jerry Bridges**

When a Christian has a healthy conscience, it will warn him *before* a wrong action is initiated. *During* the action one's conscience may be very quiet. But *afterward* you'll really hear from it. Words, thoughts, attitudes, and motives also come under its relentless scrutiny. Remember—this is a blessing. An active conscience fosters the self-examination which marks a growing Christian. It is a tremendous ally for truth.

As mentioned above, the chief danger is that we fail to heed conscience and it becomes seared. The Christian without a clear conscience is liable to be blackmailed by the enemy. Having lost such crucial navigational equipment, he can no longer discern the right course, and runs the risk of shipwreck. This is no small thing.

But a hypersensitive conscience can be as big a problem as one that has been seared. This is not unusual among serious-minded Christians, especially when they are newly converted. Those having what is sometimes called an overly scrupulous or weak conscience live in a continual state of unwarranted guilt. "Here the most insignificant little thing can produce an evil conscience, in fact, a most unbearable anxiety. It may be either an insignificant act or an unguarded little word or thought."[13] A piece of trash on the ground not picked up becomes a major sin because "anyone... who knows the good he ought to do and doesn't do it, sins" (Jas 4:17). Or an offhand comment that is not absolutely accurate becomes a premeditated lie.

As these examples illustrate, those with an overly

**For Further Study:**
To understand Paul's views on weak conscience and strong conscience, see 1 Corinthians 8:4-13 and 10:23-33.

scrupulous conscience err by exalting the letter of a Scripture verse above its spirit. Remember, God is more interested in the motive of the heart than the outward details.

It's also possible that they fail to distinguish temptation from sin. The one often leads to the other, it is true, but they are not the same. Temptation is unavoidable, but it need not give birth to sin. As Luther said, "You can't stop the birds from flying over your head, but you can keep them from building a nest in your hair."

My advice to those with a hypersensitive conscience is to seek the counsel of a mature Christian—a pastor or small group leader who can provide some help in sorting out essentials from non-essentials. Also, active involvement in your church's small group ministry is indispensable for maintaining a healthy conscience.

**4** Which of the following would you consider sins worthy of repentance? (Check all that apply.)

❑ Leaving a wad of gum under the seat in front of you at church

❑ Briefly fantasizing that your mother-in-law has moved to Nepal

❑ Making a left turn on red at the only stoplight in town at 2:47 a.m.

❑ Letting your toddler go a full week without a bath

❑ Throwing away a soda can that should have been recycled

## Prayer

Prayer is our lifeline of communication with God. Through prayer we have an avenue of approach to our heavenly Father by which we may express our gratefulness and tell him our needs. It's a multi-faceted opportunity to commune with the Creator of the universe. Consistent, persistent prayer changes us as profoundly as any other means used by the Holy Spirit.

The Bible encourages us to "pray in the Spirit on all occasions with all kinds of prayers and requests. With this in mind, be alert and always keep on praying for all the saints" (Eph 6:18). There are at least three kinds of prayer that contribute greatly to our sanctification. Let's look at them individually.

**Prayer as a cry for deliverance from sin.** It's hard to

imagine a more desperate situation than the one Jonah faced. Having disobeyed God's command to go to Nineveh, he wound up in the belly of a huge fish. Prayer was his only hope:

From inside the fish Jonah prayed to the Lord his God. He said: "In my distress I called to the Lord, and he answered me. From the depths of the grave I called for help, and you listened to my cry." (Jon 2:1-2)

No matter how dire the predicament, our first step in deliverance from sin is always toward the Lord. This step is accomplished through prayer. When I know I've sinned, the way out is not complicated—just hard. The Holy Spirit directs me to cry out for mercy, to confess my sin, and to ask for forgiveness.

God's promise is clear: "If we confess our sins, he is faithful and just and will forgive us our sins and purify us from all unrighteousness" (1Jn 1:9). The Greek word translated here as "confess" means "to say the same thing"—to agree with God that we have indeed sinned. He already knows what our sin is. He is merely waiting for us to own up to it. Once we do, he promises to forgive and purify us. I find it interesting that the basis for God's forgiving response is not his mercy, but rather his faithfulness and justice. We can submit our petitions to God confidently because of what Jesus did for us on the cross.

> " Don't just sit there by yourself or off to one side and hang your head, and shake it and gnaw your knuckles and worry and look for a way out, nothing on your mind except how bad *you* feel, how *you* hurt, what a poor guy you are. Get up, you lazy scamp! Down on your knees! Up with your hands and eyes toward heaven! [14] "
>
> — **Martin Luther**

**Meditate on Psalm 86:1-7.** Though we deserve his wrath, God is "abounding in love" when we cry out for deliverance from sin.

Prayer for deliverance from sin is a manifestation of true humility. And humility is necessary for experiencing grace.

**Prayer as a request for guidance.** I recall the period of time just before I asked my wife to marry me. Boy, was I ever serious about receiving direction from God! Just the sheer number of prayers for guidance must have impressed the Lord that I really wanted to know *his* will.

Receiving guidance involves more than prayer, of course. For instance, it requires biblical study and faithful application of the wisdom we already possess. It anticipates our having a sincere determination to do God's will no matter what, and a willingness to heed the multitude of counselors he mercifully places around us. But prayer is primary in guidance simply because it keeps us in constant contact with the One who guides us in paths of righteousness for his name's sake (Ps 23:3).

No one can reduce true guidance to a formula. It consists in hearing and obeying, a steady relationship reinforced by regular communication and resting on the sure promises of God. My own opinion is that a Christian intent on doing the will of God will find it difficult to miss that will if he or she is a person of prayer.

**Prayer as submission to the will of God.** In the Garden of Gethsemane, Jesus prayed the most poignant of all prayers: "Father, if you are willing, take this cup from me; yet not my will, but yours be done" (Lk 22:42). It was accompanied by strong crying out to God and a stress so intense that Christ sweated drops of blood. It was uttered when he was without human companionship, because those nearest him had fallen asleep. Our Lord was alone. Here, in his hour of greatest testing, Jesus gave us a model of true submission, a meekness that qualified him to inherit the earth.

**5** Briefly describe one incident when you received deliverance or guidance from God as a result of prayer.

Toward the end of World War II, allied aircraft pounded Germany with heavy incendiary bombs. Cities such as Dresden and Hamburg were completely leveled. One of the survivors of Dresden was John Noble, an American citizen placed under house arrest along with his family when the war broke out.[15] He was 22.

After the Axis powers surrendered in 1945, John hoped to return to America. But the Soviet Communists now controlled that part of Germany, and they had different plans for him. He was thrown in prison under a pretext and for the next ten years was subjected to some of the most inhumane treatment imaginable. Only a tiny fraction of those imprisoned survived. Those who had suffered under both the Germans and the Communists said that while the Nazis were much more cruel and vindictive in their treatment of prisoners, the Communists were more deadly, since they systematically starved most of those in their grasp.

**For Further Study:**
Read Hebrews 12:7-13. What promise do we find here that motivates us to submit to God?

Though Noble had been raised in a Christian home, his faith didn't extend much beyond superficial church attendance. Grace was said at mealtime, but prayers, if said at all, were not heartfelt. His father, a former minister, had become increasingly materialistic over the years. He took the family to Germany in the mid-thirties to run a camera factory. That's how they happened to be stuck in Germany when Hitler's troops started marching.

In the prison all captives were repeatedly denied food for long stretches of time. Then came a crushing twelve-day period with nothing except a little coffee-flavored water each day. Many of the men died. From his solitary cell, John could hear bodies being dragged out, their heads thumping on the stairs. Hopelessness and despair hung like a cloud all around. But during that period of slow, painful starvation, God graciously revealed himself to John Noble.

He had of course prayed during the earlier period of his captivity. In fact, he had prayed often, asking God for food, safety, and deliverance. When he was given faith to trust in Christ, however, the focus of his prayers changed from self-preservation to a humble submission to the will of God. Now, whether he lived or died, he was submitted to God. He was no longer his own. As a result, he was no longer fearful. A peace surpassing human comprehension settled over his soul.

John's father, a fellow inmate in the Dresden prison, also rededicated his life to Christ and received the same grace to pray, "Not my will but yours be done." While they were to spend several more years in prison, they later wrote of having no regrets. They never felt spiritually richer or closer to Christ than when, naturally speaking, things seemed most grim. And their trust in Jesus, which was so precious to them, empowered them to reclaim the miserable lives of many others. Throughout their ordeal, the humble prayer of submission to the will of God kept their hearts tender and close to him.

As you can see, prayer—together with God's Word and a regenerated conscience—are powerful tools in the Spirit's hand. They have amazing potential for conforming us to the image of Christ. Now that you've gotten some idea of how these work, let's rummage through the rest of the toolbox. ∎

**Meditate on Philippians 1:20-21.** Once again, Paul serves as a perfect role model. What was his one concern as he faced the likelihood of execution?

> ❝ Prayer will make a man cease from sin, or sin will entice a man to cease from prayer.[16] ❞
>
> — John Bunyan

**GROUP DISCUSSION**

1. Martin Luther once said, "A man is justified by faith alone, but not by a faith that is alone." How might that apply to the author's pre-conversion questions about smoking? (Pages 53-54)

2. What sins would you consider to be among the most controlling or addictive? Why?

3. Can you recall specific ways in which the Holy Spirit worked to sanctify you after your conversion?

4. How is your expectation of change affected by the knowledge that God himself is working in you?

5. Think of an underground cave, hollowed out over centuries by the steady trickle of water. At the rate God's Word is "trickling" into your life now, how long will it take to produce visible change?

6. What would it take to insure that you are reading—and applying—God's Word on a regular basis?

7. How would you rate your conscience? (A) Too callous, (B) Too sensitive, (C) Just right

8. "When I know I've sinned," says the author, "the way out is not complicated—just hard" (Page 64). Why is it difficult to pray for God's deliverance?

9. "Prayer Changes Things" announces a familiar billboard. In what ways have you found that to be true in your life?

**RECOMMENDED READING**

*Tabletalk*, a monthly Bible study guide published by Ligonier Ministries, 400 Technology Park, Suite 150, Lake Mary, Florida, 32746, 1-800-435-4343)

*Daily Walk*, a monthly Bible study guide published by Walk Thru the Bible Ministries, P.O. Box 478, Mt. Morris, IL 61054-9887.

*Daily Readings from J.C. Ryle*, compiled by Robert Sheehan (Welwyn, Hertfordshire, England: Evangelical Press, 1982)

*How to Pray Effectively* by Wayne Mack (Phillipsburg, NJ: Presbyterian & Reformed Publishing Co., 1977)

*Honesty, Morality & Conscience* by Jerry White (Colorado Springs, CO: NavPress, 1977)

# CHAPTER SIX

# TOOLS OF THE TRADE (II)

ROBIN BOISVERT

I n the previous chapter we explored three of the primary tools—Scripture, conscience, and prayer—the Holy Spirit uses to accomplish our sanctification. Yet there are at least six important means remaining. In order to respond to the Spirit's sanctifying work, we must familiarize ourselves with these other essential tools of the trade.

## Self-Denial and a Life of Discipleship

A few years ago Fritos introduced an extremely hot Jalapeno chip. I tried to conceal my pleasure that, since the kids couldn't stand them, I wouldn't have to share.

At the store my children would ask, "Hey, Dad, why are we getting that kind? We don't like them!" *I know*, thought I. *That is precisely the point.*

Within months, Fritos discontinued that flavor...no doubt on orders from above.

The famous Chinese Christian leader Watchman Nee once wrote, "Let us remember that the one reason for all misunderstanding, all fretfulness, all discontent, is that we secretly love ourselves."[1] I can only add that with some of us, it's no secret. We may attempt to hide our selfishness, but it inevitably bubbles up to the surface. Far better to heed Jesus' call and address this self-love directly.

**Meditate on John 15:13.** What is the measure of true love?

> Then he said to them all: "If anyone would come after me, he must deny himself and take up his cross daily and follow me. For whoever wants to save his life will lose it, but whoever loses his life for me will save it." (Lk 9:23-24)

Each day in Christ's school of discipleship holds fresh opportunity for self-denial. Why is this much-forgotten key to the Christian life so important? Because it overcomes selfishness, making it possible for us to love God and others.

One arena in which selfishness gets exposed pretty quickly is marriage. I have often said to my wife (only half facetiously), "Honey, it's not that I don't love you. My problem is that I just love myself more." Fortunately, God provides us with a custom-fitted cross for the removal of such attitudes.

> **There is within each of us an enemy which we tolerate at our peril. Jesus called it 'life' and 'self,' or as we would say, the *self-life*. To allow this enemy to live is, in the end, to lose everything. To repudiate it and give up all for Christ's sake is to lose nothing at last, but to preserve everything unto life eternal.**[2]
>
> **— A.W. Tozer**

Don't be fooled by the psychobabble that teaches we must first learn to love ourselves in order to become whole. Nowhere in Scripture are we commanded to love ourselves. We love ourselves too much as it is. In fact, we give ourselves the benefit of the doubt in almost every possible instance. We blame conflicts on others while flattering ourselves for having noble intentions. If we only extended to others the same grace we grant ourselves... what a wonderful world it would be.

**For Further Study:**
What is the underlying assumption of Paul's exhortation in Ephesians 5:28-33?

When Jesus said one of the requirements for eternal life was to "love your neighbor as yourself," he was not suggesting that self-love was in any way deficient. Rather, he was saying "love your neighbor as you (already) love yourself"—and that's a whole lot of loving. But it will not come naturally. It may be one of the most unnatural things you ever do. Loving others comes only as we practice self-denial along the pathway of discipleship.

Self-denial and love intersect at the point of serving. Jesus gave us the supreme example by going to the cross on our behalf. That was the ultimate act of selfless service. But all during his life he put the needs and welfare of others before his own. Whether washing his disciples' feet or feeding hungry multitudes, our Lord led by example. In Philippians 2, Paul could point to Jesus' serving, self-denying attitude as one all Christians should emulate.

**1** Think of one person you know well who has a specific need. How could you sacrificially serve him or her during the next week?

Each of you should look not only to your own interests, but also to the interests of others. Your attitude should be the same as that of Christ Jesus: Who, being in

> **""** Self-denial awaits the sons of God as they enter upon their private devotions. It stands at the threshold of witnessing and other service to our holy Lord. It is a most painful element in each struggle after holiness. Denial of self is the key to the solution of numerous practical questions which perplex the sober-minded believer of today. A right understanding of this basic biblical demand would silence a host of errors regarding evangelism, sanctification and practical living.[3] **""**
>
> — **Walter Chantry**

very nature God, did not consider equality with God something to be grasped, but made himself nothing, taking the very nature of a servant.... (Php 2:4-7)

Another book in this series, *Disciplines for Life*, discusses in detail the various biblical ways we may practice a life of discipleship. Spiritual exercises such as fasting, consistent prayer, and confession require effort. But they are well worth it, promising rewards now and in the life to come.

## Trials Along the Way

It was one of Job's counselors who accurately surmised, "Man is born to trouble as surely as sparks fly upward" (Job 5:7). That's been our lot ever since the Fall. Many of those difficulties, of course, result from our own sin and foolishness. On more than one occasion I've traced a headache to tension caused by my own stubborn persistence in worry. When Clara and I experience friction in our marriage, more likely than not my selfishness is to blame. We shouldn't be surprised when we suffer the consequences of our sinful behavior. However, the Lord can graciously use even these for our growth in godliness if we will repent and seek to learn from them.

But what about those trials—those Joseph scenarios—for which we are not responsible? It's unlikely we'll be sold into slavery by our family members, but there are times when others sin against us, or when we suffer afflictions just because we live in a fallen world.

Joseph saw the big picture. He recognized his eternal destiny and the destinies of those around him. Consequently, he was able to appreciate the way God sovereignly directed his life's circumstances. As he told his brothers, "You intended to harm me, but God intended it for good to accomplish what is now being done, the saving of many lives" (Ge 50:20).

When things seem to go against us, we must realize our Father has a purpose in mind and is primarily interested in our response. As a matter of fact, it's not too much to say God engineers difficulties in order to urge us onward in dependent trust upon him:

Remember how the Lord your God led you all the way in the desert these forty years, to humble you and to test you in order to know what was in your heart, whether or not you would keep his commands. He humbled you, causing you to hunger and then feeding you with manna, which neither you nor your fathers had known, to teach you that man does not live on bread alone but on every word that comes from the mouth of the Lord. (Dt 8:2-3)

Who humbled and tested the Israelites, bringing them to a place of hunger? Was it Satan? No—it was God. Why? So they would know how much they needed an ongoing, vital relationship with him. Pause a moment to let this sink in: God is prepared to sacrifice your short-term happiness in order to achieve his eternal and gracious purpose in you. As a genuine Christian, you "must go through many hardships to enter the kingdom of God" (Ac 14:22). Don't confuse your Father's loving discipline for cruelty or neglect.

**For Further Study:**
Why did God ask Abraham to sacrifice Isaac (Genesis 22:1-18)? What emotions do you think Abraham experienced as he set out to obey God?

> ❝ We lose a lot of comfort in times of trials because we tend to view them as evidences of God's desertion of us rather than evidences of his Fatherly discipline and care. Hebrews 12:7, however, says, 'Endure hardship as discipline; God is treating you as sons.' The writer of Hebrews did not qualify hardship. He did not suggest that *some* hardship is God's discipline, while some may not be. He simply said endure hardship—all of it— as God's discipline. You may be sure that whatever hardship comes into your life from whatever immediate source, God is in sovereign control of it and is using it as an instrument of discipline in your life.[4] ❞
>
> — **Jerry Bridges**

Joseph learned what we all must learn: "in all things God works for the good of those who love him, who have been called according to his purpose" (Ro 8:28). Not some things, or even most things. All things. Even in cases of rape or childhood sexual abuse or birth defects or terminal illness, the sovereign God always has a redemptive plan that will lead to his greater glory.

To understand Paul's statement here, we must focus on God's agenda, not our own. His purpose is that we be conformed to the image of his Son. Thus, hardships or injustices—though not seemingly favorable to us—qualify as "good" because they serve to make us more like Christ.

**Meditate on 1 Peter 1:6-7.** Here's a way to look at suffering that will help you endure even the most difficult trials.

This is not easy to accept or understand. I wouldn't fault you for asking, "But how can Paul claim that *all* things work together for my good? I see many things working for me, but many others that seem to be working against me." Let me try to answer that with an illustration.

Before the advent of digital timepieces, a watch's inner workings consisted of a number of cogs, some turning in a clockwise direction and others counter-clockwise. At first glance it might seem unlikely that anything useful could result from such an arrangement. But when the mainspring was wound, though the wheels turned in opposite directions, they all worked together to move the hands of the watch forward.

So it is with God's providential ordering of the universe ...and of our lives.[5] We need to realize God is so interested in our spiritual growth (sanctification) that he is willing to sacrifice our temporal happiness to secure eternal blessings for us.

It's easy to be a Christian when things are going well. But in the heat of difficult circumstances, some doubt they will be able to maintain their allegiance to Christ. Often, as a young Christian, I would read of Peter's denial of Christ and wonder if I would someday do the same. Perhaps you've had similar thoughts. The fact is, however, that Jesus prayed for Peter and through grace restored him to a place of great usefulness.

The reason we persevere as Christians is because God himself preserves us:

**2** "From Trial To Triumph" is a consistent biblical theme. Using the Bible reference next to each of the Trials" listed below, fill in the ultimate victory each of these individuals experienced.

| Trial | Triumph |
|---|---|
| • Man blind from birth **(John 9:3)** | • |
| • Christians persecuted in Jerusalem **(Acts 8:1,4)** | • |
| • Elizabeth's barren womb **(Luke 1:5-7, 13-17)** | • |
| • Jesus' crucifixion **(Philippians 2:8-11)** | • |
| • Abraham's call to sacrifice Isaac **(Genesis 22:15-18)** | • |

My sheep listen to my voice; I know them, and they follow me. I give them eternal life, and they shall never perish; *no one can snatch them out of my hand.* My Father, who has given them to me, is greater than all; no one can snatch them out of my Father's hand. I and the Father are one. (Jn 10:27-30, emphasis added)

It is hard to imagine a more emphatic and reassuring declaration of protection.

**Meditate on 1 Peter 1:3-5.** God himself promises to shield us with his power until the end.

> **「** Christ's petitions call down such aid to faith that it stands even in its darkest hour. Whenever we find our lives drawn into the snares of the devil as Peter did, we cannot rely on our own strength, nor even on our own faith, but only upon Christ's faithfulness in prayer for his weak brethren. That knowledge brings consolation. It also brings assurance that nothing will ever separate us from God's love in Christ.[6] **」**
>
> — **Sinclair Ferguson**

"The doctrine [of perseverance] declares that the regenerate are saved through persevering in faith and Christian living to the end, and that it is God who keeps them persevering," writes J.I. Packer.[7] God's Word tells us that Jesus Christ saves "to the uttermost" everyone who comes to God by him (Heb 7:25 NKJV).

Thus, every Christian may have assurance that he or she will persevere, not because of any individual's own strength or ability, but because God is faithful to preserve us.

### The Place of the Law

Christians are often confused about the role God's law has in sanctification. I've heard some people loudly proclaim, without any qualification, that the law has been done away with—and good riddance. And I've heard just the opposite from others whose agenda for reforming society includes the wholesale re-institution of Old Testament law, administered much as Islamic law is enforced in some fundamentalist Moslem countries today. As I see it, neither extreme does justice to the New Testament's teaching on the subject.

Before we go any further, though, let's clarify what we mean by "the law." I'm indebted to theologian Bruce Milne for the following description:

> By "law" is here meant the fundamental Old Testament moral prescriptions summarized in the decalogue [Ten Commandments]. Old Testament ceremonial laws have been superseded in the sense that Christ has fulfilled them; Old Testament social legislation ceased to be normative in the sense that the church has replaced the theocracy of Israel. Principles underlying both ceremonial and social laws have continuing relevance and application.[8]

Milne's definition represents the distillation of a great deal of closely reasoned theological study. It makes important distinctions between the use of the law now and the way it was applied during the Old Testament era. It also takes into account the utter significance of the person and work of our Lord, whose coming, though in accord with the law, resulted in a thoroughly new awareness of what that law means. Scripture shows the transition we've made from *slaves* of the law to *sons*: "But when the time had fully come, God sent his Son, born of a woman, born under law, to redeem those under law, that we might receive the full rights of sons" (Gal 4:4-5).

Milne has effectively refuted the would-be reformers seeking to institutionalize Mosaic laws, but we still need to address those who consider the law null and void. Is the law an ongoing help or an outdated hindrance?

The *un*-unequivocal answer to this question is...both. If we view the law as a means to right standing with God (justification), then we'll be hindered from true sanctification as the Pharisees were. They failed to see law-keeping was never intended to justify us, not even under the Old Covenant. On the other hand, if we understand God's purpose for the law, then it remains a useful tool in our pursuit of sanctification.

The law has always represented the character of God, reflecting his interest in holiness. And the Ten Commandments still serve as the effective summary of God's moral and ethical expectations of the human race.

Let's pose another fundamental question: Why did God give these "moral prescriptions" in the first place? If the law was never intended to justify us, what is its purpose?

**To restrain evildoing.** According to Scripture, the "lawful use of the law" serves to curb the spread of evil (1Ti 1:9-11 NAS). Because lawlessness threatens both individual godliness and society, some check on it is essential. In this regard God's law corresponds to secular criminal law.

**To show us our sin.** "Where then lies the point of the law? It was an addition made to underline the existence and extent of sin until the arrival of the 'seed' to whom the promise referred" (Gal 3:19 Phillips). As the New English Bible puts it, the law was added "to make wrongdoing a legal offense," that is, to make men clearly aware of the distinction between good and evil. Or as William Hendriksen states, "to bring about within his heart and

> ❝ The law drives us to the Gospel. The Gospel saves us from the curse of the law but in turn directs us back to the law to search its spirit, its goodness and its beauty. The law of God is still a lamp unto our feet. Without it we stumble and trip and grope in darkness.[9] ❞
>
> — R.C. Sproul

**Meditate on 1 Timothy 1:8.** What is the big "if" in this verse?

mind an awakened sense of guilt."[10] J.B. Phillips expresses it well in his translation of the Bible: "It is the straight-edge of the law that shows us how crooked we are" (Ro 3:20). Once it has exposed our true nature, the law can accomplish its next crucial purpose.

**To bring us to Christ.** "Before this faith came," wrote Paul, "we were held prisoners by the law, locked up until faith should be revealed" (Gal 3:23). Trying to fulfill the law's demands is a futile task. And that, in fact, is the very revelation the law is intended to bring. It exists to show us our sinful, weak, and desperate condition. "Therefore the law has become our tutor to lead us to Christ, that we may be justified by faith" (Gal 3:24 NAS). Once we've battered our legalistic selves silly against the law's unyielding demands, we will be ready "to turn to God and to his Son Jesus Christ for pardon and power."[11]

**For Further Study:**
Read Deuteronomy 4:1. Why is it in our own best interest to obey the law?

**To serve as a guideline for godly living.** Like guardrails along a highway, the law is designed to keep us from going off course. It also clarifies the course we ought to pursue. *Torah*, the Hebrew word for "law," has several meanings, including "the sort of instruction a good parent gives his child."[12] God as our Father wants to spare us unnecessary difficulties. If we want to live smart, we'll keep his law.

Once we come to Christ, our relationship to the law changes radically. Our motive for obeying its decrees is no longer fear but gratitude. When we realize that the God who created, redeems, and sustains us with unmerited grace is worthy of our joyful obedience, we will say with the psalmist, "Oh, how I love your law!" (Ps 119:97).

**3** Loving God's law is one thing; loving Uncle Sam's laws is another. Which of the following laws did you love before you became a Christian? How about now? (Check all that apply.)

| Non-Christian | | Christian |
|---|---|---|
| ❏ | Must not exceed the posted speed limit | ❏ |
| ❏ | Must report all taxable income | ❏ |
| ❏ | Must not sell alcohol to minors | ❏ |
| ❏ | Must wear a seatbelt | ❏ |

Those who consider the law outdated and irrelevant pose a number of questions worth answering:

"But hasn't the law ended?"

Only as a means to righteousness. "Christ is the end [goal, completion] of the law so that there may be righteousness for everyone who believes" (Ro 10:4).

"Didn't Paul say we 'are not under law' (Ro 6:14)?"

It's true that we are now under grace, not law, as the controlling force in our lives. But what Paul meant is that "we are no longer under condemnation because of our failure to keep the law."[13]

"Didn't Jesus abolish the law?"

Not at all. "Do not think that I have come to abolish the Law or the Prophets; I have not come to abolish them but to fulfill them" (Mt 5:17). "What Jesus destroyed," writes J.I. Packer, "was inadequate expositions of the law, not the law itself (Matthew 5:21-48; 15:1-9; etc.). By giving truer expositions, he actually republished the law."[14] Jesus clarified the spirit of the law, saying in effect, "No adultery, not even in thought. No murder, not even hate."

It is the Christian's great privilege to be free from the law. However, we must not interpret this as a disparaging commentary on the law. The fault is not with the law but with us; it is weak because our flesh is weak. But fortunately, what we were unable to do, God did for us.

> For what the law was powerless to do in that it was weakened by the sinful nature, God did by sending his own Son in the likeness of sinful man to be a sin offering. And so he condemned sin in sinful man, in order that the righteous requirements of the law *might be fully met in us* who do not live according to the sinful nature but according to the Spirit. (Ro 8:3-4, emphasis added)

We can sum up our discussion as follows: The law is still in effect and serves a valuable purpose, but through Christ our status under the law has forever changed. God's role in our lives is now primarily that of Father, not Judge. When we sin we grieve him and are disciplined, but we are not disowned. His dealings with us are now the chastening love of a father, not the legal disapproval of a judge.

## The Church

The Christian life is inescapably corporate. The idea of a holy man or woman apart from a holy church is foreign

> 66 Is the law still binding upon the Christian?... 'No' in the sense that our acceptance before God does not depend on it. Christ in his death fully met the demands of the law, so that we are delivered from it. It no longer has any claims on us. It is no longer our lord. 'Yes' in the sense that our new life is still a bondage. We still 'serve.' We are still slaves, although discharged from the law. But the motive and the means of our service have altered.
>
> Why do we serve? Not because the law is our master and we have to, but because Christ is our husband and we want to. Not because obedience to the law leads to salvation, but because salvation leads to obedience to the law. The law says, Do this and you will live. The gospel says, You live, so do this. The motive has changed.[15] 99
>
> — John R.W. Stott

**Meditate on Romans 10:4.** Through our union with Christ, we have fully met the righteous requirements of the law.

77

to the New Testament. And yet a large majority of Americans today think they can serve God just as effectively apart from the community of believers. In the words of one Gallup poll respondent, "I am my own church."

One of the unfortunate consequences of American "rugged individualism" is an independent streak that keeps many from forming the lasting relationships that characterize the church. Resistance to commitment in the name of freedom results in stunted spiritual growth.

Then there is the fear that paralyzes people the moment they consider church involvement:

"What if they find out what I am really like?"

"Everybody but me has his or her life in order."

"I'm not like everybody else."

I've heard comments like these so often I can say with confidence that every church member has (or had) similar thoughts. The answer to such fears is that the church is composed of imperfect people who, with God's help, are learning to follow him. No one has "arrived." Are you imperfect? Great! You'll fit right in.

> ❝ The Bible knows nothing of solitary religion. Sir, you wish to serve God and go to heaven? Remember, you cannot serve God alone. You must therefore find companions or make them. ❞
>
> — John Wesley

Selfishness is another problem that keeps people isolated from the fellowship of the church. Some folks are just too into themselves to be bothered with caring about anyone else. But the simple fact is, we need each other. "One cannot claim to be a Christian," writes Charles Colson, "and at the same time claim to be outside the church. To do so is at the least hypocrisy—at the worst, blasphemy."[16] Sanctification can only be worked out in the context of Christian community.

There is no substitute for the encouragement and admonishment that comes from faithful brothers and sisters in the church. The New Testament contains thirty "one another" passages showing the importance of shared lives. Besides, we all benefit from people who demonstrate faith in action, showing us how to be good husbands, wives, parents, friends, or workers. As mentioned in the previous chapter, taking part in a small group where you can know and be known is very important.

In addition to all this, it is to the Church that Christ has given the gifts of apostles, prophets, evangelists, pastors and teachers. Why? To equip the saints so the saints can fulfill the work of ministry to which they are called

**For Further Study:**
Read 1 Thessalonians 5:4-11. How does the last verse in this passage reinforce Paul's call to live as "sons of the light"?

4

What are two (at least!) of the "indispensable" benefits you've gained by being involved in a local church?

•

•

(Eph 4:11-13). God provides spiritual leadership for Christians within the local church. It is in the church that we receive pastoral care and are trained to serve. We may thank God for parachurch ministries and the good they do, but they are not indispensable. The Church is.

## The Sacraments

If you grew up attending church services, you are probably familiar with the sacraments. Though Christian traditions disagree on the number or practice of the sacraments, there are two—baptism and communion—that have always been regarded as distinctively Christian and central to the life of the Church. These two are equally essential in the life of each believer.

A sacrament is really a promise of God acted out before our eyes.[17] We are told that our sins are washed away by the blood of the Lamb. But then we are invited to give evidence of our faith in that promise by following Christ through the waters of baptism. Likewise, we are promised eternal life and fellowship with Jesus, and then allowed to commune with him as we receive the Lord's own supper.

There is no magic in these acts. Baptism does not make one a Christian. Rather, only Christians qualify to be baptized. Nor is saving grace imparted through communion. Yet Christ is certainly present by his Spirit as we remember his broken body and shed blood.

These ordinances have great value for our sanctification. They are vivid experiential reminders of the great truths of the Christian faith—our redemption through the finished work of Jesus Christ and our abiding fellowship with him until he returns for us. Or, as Sinclair Ferguson has put it, they bring "fresh realization of our union and communion with Christ. They point us back to its foundation and forward to its consummation in glory."[18] The sacraments keep these truths front and center, helping us maintain the firm footing essential for spiritual growth.

## Worship and Praise

Recently I attended a conference on biblical counseling. Though the opening prayer was far from perfunctory, none of us were particularly moved. The next day's session, however, began with worship. This time when the leader prayed before starting his message, verbal praise, lifted hands, and scattered "Amens" punctuated his every phrase. What was the difference? Worship had directed our hearts upward and softened us to the Spirit of God.

Among our great privileges as Christians, none is greater than the privilege of worship. Its power to restore perspective can hardly be overestimated. How easy it is in this fallen world to "get out of tune," to lose touch with the greatness and mercy of God. Self-confidence on one hand and discouragement on the other can keep us from seeing our exalted Lord. But when we begin to worship…when his Spirit lifts our eyes to behold again the majesty and wonder of God…we are brought back into contact with eternal realities. Also, in magnifying God we invariably humble ourselves, and that puts us in a perfect position to receive grace. We would each do well to echo the hymn writer who said, "Come Thou Fount of every blessing, tune my heart to sing your praise."

Psalm 95 provides us with a wonderful pattern for worship and an understanding of its role in sanctification:

**For Further Study:**
What did Elisha's servant see when God lifted his vision above his circumstances?
(2 Kings 6:15-17)

Come, let us sing for joy to the Lord; let us shout aloud to the Rock of our salvation. Let us come before him with thanksgiving and extol him with music and song…Come, let us bow down in worship, let us kneel before the Lord our Maker; for he is our God and we are the people of his pasture, the flock under his care. Today, if you hear his voice, do not harden your hearts… (Ps 95:1-2,6-8)

**5** Take a minute or two to read Psalm 77 and then answer the following questions:

• How is the psalmist's heart out of tune (v.2,4,7-9)?

• How does he deal with his doubts (vv.10-12)?

• How does worship change his view of God (vv.13-20)?

After inviting us to sing, shout, thank, and extol, the psalmist urges us to bow in worship. He also warns us not to harden our hearts when we hear God's voice. The connection is not merely coincidental: God frequently speaks to our hearts as we worship. He tells us of his majesty, his sovereignty over our lives, his providential care for us, and many other wonderful things. He may also reveal specific areas where we need to change or venture into new realms. If we fail to listen, or if we harden our hearts as Israel did so often during her wilderness

> **❝** The fuel of worship is a true vision of the greatness of God; the fire that makes the fuel burn white-hot is the quickening of the Holy Spirit; the furnace made alive and warm by the flame of truth is our renewed spirit; and the resulting heat of our affections is powerful worship, pushing its way out in confessions, longings, acclamations, tears, songs, shouts, bowed heads, lifted hands and obedient lives.[19] **❞**
>
> — John Piper

wanderings, we risk God's displeasure and discipline.

As a pastor, I am keenly aware of the struggles people face throughout the week, and of my own limitations in helping them. But when we gather as a church to worship on Sunday mornings, I see how consistently God uses these times to shepherd his people. The discouraged, the lonely, and the fearful all find God's strong and tender hands there to uphold them as they worship him.

I don't think there is a more effective pastoral strategy for helping people than leading them into the place of worship where God himself can minister to them. In the place of worship, lives are changed. ■

**GROUP DISCUSSION**
1. What is one especially sacrificial thing you've done for someone else?

2. "We love ourselves too much as it is," says the author. (Page 70) Do you agree or disagree?

3. Describe one trial you experienced which ultimately turned out for good.

4. What specific benefits may result from trials you are facing right now?

5. Did this chapter change the way you think of the law? Explain.

6. What was the law never intended to do? (Page 75)

7. In response to your invitation to attend church, your neighbor says (with just a trace of arrogance), "I am my *own* church." How would you answer?

8. Read aloud the quote by John Piper on this page. Why ⁻ ⌐bedient lives a natural byproduct of worship?

**RECOMMENDED** *Disciplines for Life* by C.J. Mahaney and John Loftness
**READING** (Gaithersburg, MD: Sovereign Grace Ministries, 1992)

*Trusting God* by Jerry Bridges (Colorado Springs, CO: NavPress, 1988)

*The Body* by Charles Colson and Ellen Santilli Vaughn (Dallas, TX: Word, Inc., 1992)

*Desiring God* by John Piper (Portland, OR: Multnomah Press, 1986)

*In the Shadow of the Cross: Studies in Self-Denial* by Walter J. Chantry (Carlisle, PA: Banner of Truth, 1981)

# CHAPTER SEVEN

# LIVING FOR THAT FINAL DAY

C.J. MAHANEY

When was the last time you heard a sermon about hell? Heaven is a much more popular subject, but even that is often ignored these days. The trend in contemporary preaching is to focus not on our eternal future, but on our current "felt needs." And while such messages may succeed at drawing crowds, they fail to develop maturity and build the Church. Listen to this excellent observation by Darius Salter from his book *What Really Matters in Ministry*:

> Lack of rootage in the eternal may be the greatest shortcoming in the evangelical preaching that attracts large numbers of people...The ultimate aim of preaching should not be accruing benefits in this life for parishioners but preparing individuals to stand in the presence of Christ. There is no greater goal or motivation than the knowledge that all of us are headed for eternity, and that shortly.[1]

> **❝** A startling thing has happened among Western Christians. Many of us habitually think and act as if there is no eternity—or as if what we do in this present life has no bearing on eternity...Being oblivious to eternity leaves us experts in the trivial, and novices in the significant. We can name that tune, name that starting line-up, name that actor's movie debut, name that country's leading export, and detail the differences between computer models or types of four-wheel drives. None of this is wrong, of course, but it is certainly revealing when we consider that most Christians, let alone the general public, do not even have an accurate picture of what the Bible says will happen to us after we die. We major in the momentary and minor in the momentous.[2] **❞**
> — **Randy Alcorn**

If anyone was rooted in and motivated by the eternal, it was Paul. Without disregarding the practical needs of those he served, he constantly drew their attention to the life that was to come. And he tells us why in his second letter to the

Corinthians: "For we must all appear before the judgment seat of Christ, that each one may receive what is due him for the things done while in the body, whether good or bad" (2Co 5:10).

This verse reveals one of Scripture's most compelling —and most frequently overlooked—incentives for sanctification. It speaks of a day when we will be judged for the way we have lived in response to God's grace. On the basis of that assessment, Christ will give each believer "what is due him." One need not meditate for long on the implications of that verse to develop an appetite for godly living. We have one short life in which to determine our eternal rewards...or eternal loss. It's this urgency Paul sought to impart to the churches he served.

## Living by a Two-Day Calendar

> As a prisoner for the Lord, then, I urge you to live a life worthy of the calling you have received. (Eph 4:1)

Every genuine Christian has received a calling from God. This call was conceived in eternity past. Before creating the world, God had already chosen us for himself (Eph 1:4). At the moment of our regeneration we experience the effect of that choice. This isn't a result of human effort, nor is it a reward for good works—it is entirely a work of grace. And yet in response to God's call we are responsible to live a certain way.

This is an often misunderstood point, so please follow carefully: We never were and never will be worthy of this call. Paul is not exhorting us somehow to qualify for our calling. That would be impossible and a denial of grace. He describes it to the Ephesians as a calling "you have *received*"—not something they had *achieved*. The "riches of God's grace that he lavished upon us" (Eph 1:7-8) by way of election, adoption, redemption, and regeneration are unconditionally and freely given.

Every Christian needs to cultivate an assurance of and security in this calling. Yet it's our privilege and responsibility to build on that foundation through the process of sanctification. As Paul said of himself, "By the grace of God I am what I am, and his grace to me was not without effect" (1Co 15:10). Having received a calling of which we were not worthy, we are now responsible to live worthy of that calling.

Paul lived with an intense awareness that each of us will one day stand before Christ to account for the way we

**For Further Study:**
Read Ephesians 2:6-7. What does Paul say is the purpose of God's call on our lives?

**Meditate on 2 Thessalonians 1:11.**
It brings great assurance to know that God's expectations of a worthy life are met because he empowers us to live up to that call.

> **1** Read the second half of the verse mentioned above (1 Corinthians 15:10). How does Paul describe the effect grace had on him?
>
> ❑ Made him feel better about himself
>
> ❑ Helped him relax rather than feel pressured
>
> ❑ Assured him of God's acceptance
>
> ❑ Kept him from striving
>
> ❑ Motivated him to work hard for the kingdom

have responded to his call. But to some this may seem like a contradiction. If Christ has forgiven us and accepts us, what's this about judgment?

As Christians, we will not be judged for our sins on the day of judgment. Jesus Christ has already been judged in our place. Because of his substitutionary sacrifice on our behalf we have been saved from the wrath of God. "Since we have now been justified by [Christ's] blood, how much more shall we be saved from God's wrath through him!" (Ro 5:9; see also Ro 8:1).

But will we be judged for the works we have done—or left undone—since conversion? Definitely. Every one of us will give an account to God and have our lives evaluated. Paul presents this in vivid terms:

**Meditate on Job 34:11-12.** How do rewards—both good and bad—reveal the justice of God?

If any man builds on this foundation [Jesus Christ] using gold, silver, costly stones, wood, hay or straw, his work will be shown for what it is, because the Day will bring it to light. It will be revealed with fire, and the fire will test the quality of each man's work...If it is burned up, he will suffer loss; he himself will be saved, but only as one escaping through the flames. (1Co 3:12-13,15)

It's critical that we grasp this distinction. Though our *reconciliation* to God has been secured, our *rewards* (or loss thereof) will be determined by the extent to which we've pursued godliness in response to his call. Not that God is obligated to reward us—this, too, is an act of sheer grace, as Jerry Bridges describes so well:

This is the amazing story of God's grace. God saves us by his grace and transforms us more and more into the likeness of his Son by his grace. In all our trials and afflictions, he sustains and strengthens us by his grace. He calls us by grace to perform our own unique function within the Body of Christ. Then, again by grace, he gives to each of us the spiritual gifts necessary to fulfill our calling. As we serve him, he makes that service acceptable to himself by grace, and then rewards us a hundredfold by grace.[3]

**For Further Study:** What compelling motivation did Moses and Jesus have in common? (See Hebrews 11:26, 12:2)

But I think it's safe to say that most Christians have the attitude, *If I can just get past the box office I'll be set for eternity.* They assume everybody will wind up in "General Seating." But that's just not biblical. Scripture clearly teaches that rewards will vary. To overlook this truth is to neglect one of the main incentives for sanctification.

Martin Luther said there were only two days on his calendar: "today" and "*that* Day."[4] Each day brings us closer to *that* Day. It will be a day of unparalleled rejoicing as we see our Lord face to face. But it will also be a day of intense scrutiny and examination. And as Randy Alcorn explains, "It is we, by virtue of our hourly and daily choices, who will determine what transpires on that day."[5]

> **"** There will be great rewards, lesser rewards, and—for some—no reward. Hence there will be much diversity, even though all will share in the blessedness of the world to come. Such is the grace and justice of the good Lord.[6] **"**
>
> — **J. Rodman Williams**

God will ask, "In light of the call you received, in light of the grace I extended despite your unworthiness, where did you invest your life? What were your priorities and values? Did you serve me or use me? Did you live a life worthy of your calling?" Again, our answers to those questions won't determine our reconciliation to God, but they will have everything to do with whether or not we receive the rewards God so eagerly desires to give us.

Randy Alcorn writes about this rarely considered subject in his excellent book *Money, Possessions and Eternity.* I find his perspective extremely helpful and motivating:

> Heaven will be a wonderful place. But what we seldom consider is that at the entry point to heaven Scripture plainly tells us there is a judgment of believers that will determine for all eternity our place or status in heaven…Scripture simply does not teach what most of us seem to assume—that heaven will transform each of us into equal beings with equal possessions and equal responsibilities and equal capacities. It does not say our previous lives will be of no eternal significance. It says exactly the opposite…
>
> We have been given fair warning that there lies ahead for each of us, at the end of the term, a final examination. It will be administered by the fairest yet strictest Headmaster in the universe. How seriously we take this clear teaching of Scripture is demonstrated by how seriously we are preparing for that day.

**Meditate on Ephesians 5:16.** What critical "study habit" does this verse encourage?

86

When we took courses in college we asked ourselves and others about the teacher: "What are his
tests like? Does he take attendance? Is he a hard
grader? What does he expect in your papers?" If I'm
to do well in the course, I must know what the
instructor expects of me. We must study the course
syllabus, God's Word, to find out the answers to
these questions. And when we find out, we should
be careful to plot our lives accordingly—in light of
the long tomorrow.[7]

Our Lord's return was a day Paul eagerly anticipated.
So should we. Secure in the fact that we stand justified in
his sight, we should devote ourselves
to the good works he has prepared
beforehand, fulfilling his eternal purpose in the context of the local church.
Then we'll be able to share Paul's confidence that "there is in store for me
the crown of righteousness, which the
Lord, the righteous Judge, will award
to me on that day" (2Ti 4:8).

But crowns come at a cost. Paul had
lived worthy of his calling. Let's now
look at someone who did not.

**2** How might God's final exam differ
from the testing procedures
common at universities today?

❑ We won't be graded on a curve

❑ We won't be able to cheat

❑ We won't be able to appeal our grade

❑ We won't be able to cram

❑ All of the above

## The Wisest Fool

It can be quite sobering to examine the private lives of
prominent figures. After studying one hundred of the
most well-known leaders in Scripture, author Robert
Clinton found that fewer than 25% of them finished life's
course with their reputation and leadership intact.
Perhaps the most tragic of those failures was Solomon.

Solomon started off with such potential and promise.
Soon after his birth, the prophet Nathan announced that
God had a specific and special name for him: Jedidiah,
meaning "loved by God" (2Sa 12:25). Every time someone
used his special nickname it was a fresh reminder of God's
affection. (You can guess that Solomon's brothers and sisters at times found it difficult growing up with him.)

As David's successor, Solomon inherited the throne of
a thriving kingdom. Initially he displayed genuine humility. One night after he sacrificed a thousand burnt offerings, God appeared to him in a dream and said, "Ask for
whatever you want me to give you." Solomon, aware of his
limitations as well as his responsibilities, responded, "I am

only a little child and do not know how to carry out my duties…So give your servant a discerning heart to govern your people and to distinguish between right and wrong. For who is able to govern this great people of yours?" (1Ki 3:7-9). God was so pleased with the request that he promised to make Solomon the wisest man (other than Jesus) in history *and* to prosper and honor him above all other kings. With God's anointing, Solomon was able to lead Israel into unprecedented and unparalleled prosperity.

But in the final analysis, Solomon squandered his call. How unprepared we are for Scripture's final assessment of his life:

**For Further Study:**
Read Hebrews 6:7-8. What will become of the person who soaks up God's grace without bearing fruit?

The Lord became angry with Solomon because his heart had turned away from the Lord…So the Lord said to Solomon, "Since this is your attitude and you have not kept my covenant and my decrees, which I commanded you, I will most certainly tear the kingdom away from you and give it to one of your subordinates." (1Ki 11:9,11)

What happened? How could a man with Solomon's unique calling bring upon himself such strong discipline? The Bible doesn't leave us speculating: "His heart was not fully devoted to the Lord his God, as the heart of David his father had been" (1Ki 11:4). Though loved, called, and uniquely gifted by God, Solomon developed a pattern of disobedience that led to his gradual, spiritual deterioration. He failed to heed his own wise counsel: "Above all else, guard your heart, for it is the wellspring of life" (Pr 4:23).

In the mercy of God, Solomon repented before he died.

**3** Solomon let his many wives lead his heart astray (1Kings 11:3). Is there anything preventing your heart from being fully devoted to the Lord your God?

But God's forgiveness couldn't relieve the agony of regret as he pondered what his life could and should have been.

His reflections are recorded in the Book of Ecclesiastes, the painful memoirs of an old man who realized much of his life had been spent in vain. Rather than live worthy of his calling, Solomon pursued every form of personal pleasure (Ecc 2:10) and found it failed to deliver as advertised. There is much we can learn from his final words:

Now all has been heard; here is the conclusion of the matter: Fear God and keep his commandments, for this is the whole duty of man. For God will bring every deed into judgment, including every hidden thing, whether it is good or evil. (Ecc 12:13-14)

**Meditate on Hebrews 6:11-12.** An early lead in the race of faith is no guarantee of success; it's how you finish that counts.

As Solomon prepared to die, I believe he was painfully aware he would not hear the words, "Well done." Only those who have done well will. But his life has been preserved as a warning so that we might avoid a similar experience. There is no reason for us to end our lives with regret. By committing our lives to the process of sanctification, we can prove to be wiser than Solomon.

## How to Ask the Right Questions

One day we will stand before God—not as a group, but alone. He will then evaluate all that's transpired in our lives since conversion. Scripture gives us a preview of that moment: "He will bring to light what is hidden in darkness and expose the motives of men's hearts. At that time each will receive his praise from God" (1Co 4:5).

God is eager to present eternal rewards to each of us. To make this possible, he has called us and regenerated us, prepared good works for us to walk in, and placed us in the local church where we can apply and obey biblical teaching. However, we must be aware that he is a just God...and an objective grader. When that day comes, there will be no second opportunity.

> **“** In most graphic terms, on the day of judgment God will ask, 'What did you do?' He will not ask, 'What happened to you?'[9] **”**
>
> — **David Powlison**

History tells us of an individual who *did* receive a second chance. Randy Alcorn relates the story:

**Meditate on 1 Corinthians 3:8.** Can you find the phrase in this verse which indicates how we will be rewarded?

Alfred Nobel was a Swedish chemist who made his fortune by inventing dynamite and other powerful explosives, which were bought by governments to produce weapons. When Nobel's brother died, one newspaper accidentally printed Alfred's obituary instead. He was described as a man who became rich from enabling people to kill each other in unprecedented quantities. Shaken from this assessment, Nobel resolved to use his fortune to reward accomplishments that benefited humanity, including what we now know as the Nobel Peace Prize.

Nobel had a rare opportunity—to look at the assessment of his life at its end, but to still be alive and have opportunity to change that assessment.

Let us put ourselves in Nobel's place. Let us read our own obituary, not as written by uninformed or biased men, but as an onlooking angel might write it from heaven's point of view. Look at it carefully. Then let us use the rest of our lives to edit that obituary into what we really want it to be.[10]

Editing our obituaries begins with the willingness to ask some penetrating questions. In fact, every day of our lives should be marked by probing biblical assessment:

"Is my knowledge of and passion for God growing?"

"Am I regularly practicing the spiritual disciplines?"

"Can others confirm that I'm growing in character?"

"Am I committed and serving in the local church?"

"Is this activity worthy of the call I have received?"

"What am I doing that's making an eternal difference?"

No decision or activity should be exempt from this kind of questioning. "The reality of our eternal future should dominate and determine the character of our present life, right down to the words we speak and the actions we take," writes Alcorn.[11] If God is going to evaluate every aspect of our lives, so should we. This will transform the way we view work, leisure, church involvements, and relationships. And it will insure that a lot less goes up in flames on that final day.

> **It ought to be the business of every day to prepare for our last day.**[12]
>
> **— Matthew Henry**

The writer of Hebrews exhorts us to "consider how we may spur one another on toward love and good deeds. Let us not give up meeting together, as some are in the habit of doing, but let us encourage one another—and all the more as you see the Day approaching" (Heb 10:24-25). I trust this chapter has enabled you to see the Day that is inevitably approaching. And we pray this book has encouraged and provoked you in the process of sanctification.

**Meditate on Revelation 22:12,14.**
Like Martin Luther, let's make this the most important day on our calendar...and start to live accordingly.

It's not an easy way you have chosen. Sanctification will be difficult, challenging, and painful—though nothing like the pain of God's disapproval. But when the Day comes and you hear God say, "Well done," all sacrifice will pale in light of your eternal reward. Compared to that, nothing else really matters.

Nothing. ■

**GROUP DISCUSSION**

1. Darius Salter writes, "The preacher who best equips his hearers to cope with the pressures of American society may not be the preacher who best prepares his people for heaven."[13] Divide the group into two parts: the "Earthly Minded" and the "Heavenly Minded." Let each group come up with three relevant sermon titles which reflect its perspective, and then compare notes.

2. How can we show God we are worthy of his calling? (Warning: This is a trick question.)

3. Should we be afraid to appear before the Judgment Seat of Christ?

4. Before reading this chapter, did you think everybody in heaven would wind up in "General Seating"? Explain.

5. What's the difference between pursuing rewards and trying to earn our salvation?

6. Is it sub-spiritual to be motivated by rewards?

7. What were the highlights of your obituary? (Page 90)

8. How are you going to respond to this chapter?

**RECOMMENDED READING**   *Money, Possessions and Eternity* by Randy Alcorn (Wheaton, IL: Tyndale House, 1989)

# DIFFERENT ROADS TO HOLINESS: AN HISTORICAL OVERVIEW
*Robin Boisvert*

It's worth noting how different traditions in the Church's history have understood sanctification. In *Spiritual Companions: An Introduction to the Christian Classics*, Peter Toon identifies three different approaches to the pathway of holiness: Greek (Eastern), Medieval Western (Roman Catholic), and Protestant.

## GREEK

The Greek approach is known as deification—the imparting of the divine life into the soul from Christ through the Holy Spirit…Thus communion and union with God is the goal of salvation and is possible for human beings as they seek to lose their dependence upon the world and the flesh and are transfigured by the light of God's grace.[1]

This method can be seen in the early monastic movement. During the third century, the hermits of Egypt reacted against a moral laxity which had begun to creep into the Church. Two centuries before, the Church had been made up of Jewish and Gentile Christians whose ethical standards were quite high. But those standards began to fall as more and more people entered the Church. Add to this the deterioration of morals which accompanied the decline of the Roman Empire and one can see the problem. The world was fast becoming, in Hobbes' phrase, "nasty, brutish, and short." Not that the Church had necessarily lowered its standards. In fact, it was morally rigorous compared to today's Church. But the hermit saints left the crumbling Roman world to seek salvation in the desert.

In a sympathetic essay, Charles Kingsley describes the lives of these ascetics as consisting of

…celibacy, poverty, good deeds towards their fellow-men, self-restraint and sometimes self-torture of every kind, to atone (as far as might be) for the sins committed after baptism: and the mental food of [these] was continued meditation upon the vanity of the world, the sinfulness of the flesh, the glories of heaven, and the horrors of hell: but with these the old hermits combined—to do them justice—a personal faith in God, and a personal love for Christ, which those who sneer at them would do well to copy.[2]

To their credit, these hermits—including the great Antony—served to check the spread of worldliness among Christians, and they inspired many to a pursuit of holiness.

The extreme methods of self-denial used by some in this tradition are well documented. In the fifth century, Simon the Stylite (pillar-saint) spent the final thirty-six years of his life atop a pillar that was gradually lengthened until it reached a height of sixty feet. He was widely imitated, and actually carried on an influential ministry as a steady stream of pilgrims came to visit and enquire of him. He spawned a movement that spread from his own Antioch to "Georgia, Thrace, Macedonia, Greece and even Egypt…there were so many stylites by the seventh century, that they were treated as a special order of religion."[3] The singular point they made in confining themselves to these lofty perches was the renunciation of the world. Had solitude been their main goal, they would certainly have discovered a way to attain that without making such spectacles of themselves.

In the centuries that followed, the monastic approach to the Christian life (whether solitary or communal) spread and was considered by many to be the ideal. What slowly emerged was a two-tiered view of Christianity. The multitudes were regarded as ordinary Christians, secular in nature, who lived in and interacted with the world. Then there were those who forsook all to become monks. If you really wanted to overcome sin, know God, and be holy, it was simply assumed you would adopt the monastic lifestyle.

Interestingly, early in my ministry, a young man from Egypt came to me for counsel. Tempted as most men are by impure thoughts and desires, he insisted that the only way for him to overcome sin would be to become a monk. Apparently the tradition runs deep. But in spite of the obvious excesses, monasticism's self-denial had two unquestionable benefits: it reminded people of their mortality and heightened an awareness of the world to come.

## MEDIEVAL WESTERN

> The medieval Western approach [which has] continued in Roman Catholic thought, is that of the three ways—the purifying/cleansing of sin; the enlightening/illuminating of the mind; and the becoming one with God by grace.[4]

This is a rich tradition that spans the Church's history and has an enduring voice even among Protestant Evangelicals. Those familiar with the writings of A.W. Tozer will note the many references and allusions to such persons as Nicholas of Cusa, Bernard of Clairveaux, and John of the Cross. What stands out most in this mystical tradition is the ardent language of devotion to God and the desire for purity of heart. There is a passion for God expressed in these works that reveals a depth of longing and a richness of subjective experience. You can't read them without halting the frenetic activity that characterizes our busy lives so that you might listen to God in meditative silence. When I read works from this tradition I'm invariably led to examine my own heart toward God and repent of the shallowness I find there.

Yet despite these strengths, certain distinctives of this contemplative road to holiness ought to give us pause. Emphasis seems to be placed on seeking a direct knowledge of God. Christ's crucial role as mediator between us and the Father is generally not portrayed as clearly as it is in Scripture. In a critique of the medieval western tradition, John Calvin wrote that "Direct knowledge of God's essence is sought only by fools."[5]

Such strong language is warranted, argues Sinclair Ferguson, to safeguard the significance of Christ's atoning work. Ferguson writes,

> While the contemplative tradition places much emphasis on Christ's humanity and passion as such, Reformed Christianity places central emphasis on the transaction which took place in the Incarnate Son of God bearing the judgment of his Holy Father against man's sin. Bypass this, it insists, and there is no access to, and therefore no real knowledge of, God.[6]

With these caveats in mind, there is much to be gained from study and meditation on the writings of this tradition.

## PROTESTANT

"The Protestant approach," says Toon, "has centered on the relationship of justification and sanctification."[7] It really wasn't until the Protestant Reformation emphasized justification by grace that sanctification began to be viewed as something distinguishable from justification. But while the two doctrines are closely related, there is a great advantage in considering them separately.

How do justification and sanctification fit together? Within the Protestant framework, of course, there are a variety of views. A Lutheran perspective, for instance, sees sanctification merely as a sub-point under justification. Lutherans stress the need for a thorough understanding of justification by grace alone (seeing ourselves as God sees us) as the way to overcome sin and live in victory. Some Lutherans have been criticized for making the doctrine of justification appear more central to the Christian life than Jesus Christ.

Reformed theology points to our union with Christ as the basis for victory; it underscores the fact that he is the author and finisher of faith as well as the captain of our salvation. Because of Christ's finished work and present intercession, we are able to mortify indwelling sin and stand against the temptations of the devil. This tradition would include not only Calvin, but also the English Puritans and their heirs.

John Wesley championed yet another position, teaching a doctrine of entire sanctification (not to be confused with total perfectionism) which stressed the experiential side of truth—not just the objective, propositional side. Anyone familiar with his conversion will understand the basis for his doctrine. None of the logical arguments for faith had seemed to help him. But when Wesley encountered the living God, all that changed. Arnold Dallimore quotes from Wesley's *Journal*: "I felt my heart strangely warmed. I felt I did trust Christ, Christ alone for salvation; and an assurance was given me that he had taken away *my* sins, even *mine*, and saved *me* from the law of sin and death."[8]

Wesley's teaching and the 18th-century Methodists in the United States generated the Holiness movement in the 19th century. Adherents of this view trusted that a direct, sanctifying experience with the Holy Spirit would impart victory subsequent to salvation. And when some in the Holiness movement received the baptism in the Holy Spirit, pentecostal holiness teaching had arrived, with its emphasis on speaking in tongues.

There are many other variations on the themes just presented, but these approaches form the main outline of the Church's attempts to understand sanctification. Taken together, they illustrate the fact that not only do our minds long to be filled with truth about God so that we might obey him, but our hearts desire to experience his reality. While these traditions contain both truths to embrace and eccentricities to avoid, all of them have contributed something to the soul's quest for holiness.

For a thorough and balanced perspective on approaches to sanctification throughout Church history, I recommend *Christian Spirituality: Five Views of Sanctification*, edited by Donald L. Alexander (Downers Grove, IL: InterVarsity Press, 1988).

# THE OLD MAN AND THE FLESH

*Robin Boisvert*

Some of the terms which the apostle Paul uses in discussing the believer's relationship to sin can cause confusion. I'm speaking of terms such as "old man," "new man," "body of sin," "flesh," and others. These can be difficult to understand. Add to this the variations which modern translators have given these words and the subject can appear daunting.

We know a profound change has occurred in the life of the believer through conversion, but just how has the believer changed?

> For we know that our *old self was crucified* with him so that the body of sin might be done away with, that we should no longer be slaves to sin—because anyone who has died has been freed from sin. (Ro 6:6-7, emphasis added)

Let's begin by trying to define our terms. "Old man" (as it is translated in the King James Version and American Standard Version) is equivalent to "old self" (New International Version, New American Standard). This term refers to the unregenerate life we lived before we were converted. As John R.W. Stott has written, the old self "denotes not our old unregenerate *nature* [flesh], but our old unregenerate life. Not my lower self, but my former self. So what was crucified with Christ was not a part of me called my 'old nature', but the whole of me as I was before I was converted."[1] John Murray's definition concurs: "'Old man' is a designation of the person in his unity as dominated by the flesh and sin."[2]

It's important for us to see that the believer is not at the same time an "old self" and a "new self," alternately dominated and directed by one or the other. We are indebted again to Murray's insight:

> The old man is the unregenerate man; the new man is the regenerate man created in Christ Jesus unto good works. It is no more feasible to call the believer a new man and an old man, than it is to call him a regenerate man and an unregenerate. And neither is it warranted to speak of the believer as having in him the old man and the new man.[3]

Thus, terms like "old man," "old self," "unregenerate life," and "former self" are synonymous, all referring to the entity that was crucified with Christ.

Notice two significant grammatical features of the passage from Romans 6 cited above. First, the verb is used in the *past tense*: "our old self *was* crucified..." The crucifixion of the old self is a finished fact. Second, the verb is also *passive in voice*, meaning that the subject (our old self) is being acted upon. In other words, the crucifixion of the old self is not something we must do, but something that is done to us.

Another important concept in the biblical doctrine of sanctification has traditionally been designated by the word "flesh" (King James Version). The New International Version uses "sinful nature." According to Stott, "flesh" refers to a "lower" nature, that part of our being inclined toward rebellion against God. This is that part of you that wants to pass on a juicy bit of gossip; that urges you to take a second look at the immodest images on the television screen. "Whatever we may call this tendency ["indwelling sin,"[4] "remnants of corruption,"[5] "vestiges of sin,"[6] or "my sinful nature"[7]] we must remember that even after we have been regenerated we still have such sinful impulses, and must still fight against them as long as we live."[8]

In Romans 6:6 Paul calls our sinful nature (i.e. flesh) the "body of sin." He says our old self was crucified with Christ so that this "body of sin might be done away with..." To be "done away with" here means to be put out of action, rendered powerless. It does *not* mean to be annihilated, gone without a trace. But our sinful nature's mastery over us has been broken.

Some, not understanding the distinction between the "old self" and the "sinful nature" have gotten Romans 6:6 confused with Galatians 5:24, which also speaks of crucifixion and the believer. Consider two translations of this verse:

> Those who belong to Christ Jesus have crucified the sinful nature with its passions and desires. (Gal 5:24 NIV)

> And they that are Christ's have crucified the flesh with the affections and lusts. (Gal 5:24 KJV)

Though helpless to take anything but a passive stance in regard to the old self (Ro 6:6), we *do* have an active part to play, as the Galatians learned, in the subjugation of the flesh. Stott sums this up with characteristic clarity:

> First, we have been crucified with Christ; but then we not only have decisively crucified (i.e. repudiated) the flesh with its passions and desires, but we take up our cross *daily* and follow Christ to crucifixion (Lk 9:23). The first is a legal death, a death to the penalty of sin; the second is a moral death, a death to the power of sin. The first belongs to the past, and is unique and unrepeatable: I died (in Christ) to sin once. The second belongs to the present, and is continuous and repeatable: I die (like Christ) to self daily. It is with the first of these two that Romans 6 is concerned.[9]

And Galatians 5 is concerned with the second.

So the old self has been dealt with. In its place we have been given a new self: "Therefore, if anyone is in Christ, he is a new creation; the old has gone, the new has come!" (2Co 5:17). And while our sinful nature (the flesh, indwelling sin, etc.) is still very much with us, its dominion over us has ended.

**NOTES**

CHAPTER ONE – Caught in the Gap Trap
1. Jay E. Adams, *The Biblical View of Self-Esteem, Self-Love, Self-Image* (Eugene, OR: Harvest House Publishers, 1986), p. 78.
2. Oscar Cullman, *Christ and Time* (Philadelphia, PA: The Westminster Press, 1964), p. 3.
3. John Piper, *The Pleasures Of God* (Portland, OR: Multnomah Press, 1991), p. 147.
4. Ern Baxter, taped message, "Sanctification," n.d.
5. Quoted in *Gathered Gold*, John Blanchard, ed. (Welwyn, Hertfordshire, England: Evangelical Press, 1984), p.146.
6. J.C. Ryle, *Holiness* (Welwyn, Hertfordshire, England: Evangelical Press, 1879, reprinted 1989), p. 39.
7. Anthony A. Hoekema, *Saved by Grace* (Grand Rapids, MI: Eerdmans Publishing Co., 1989), pp. 192-93.
8. Jerry Bridges, *The Practice of Godliness* (Colorado Springs, CO: NavPress, 1983), pp. 15-20.
9. Ibid., p. 24.
10. Ibid., p. 26.
11. J.I. Packer, *Concise Theology* (Wheaton, IL: Tyndale House, 1993), p. 169.
12. R.A. Muller, *The International Standard Bible Encyclopedia, Volume Four* (Grand Rapids, MI: Eerdmans Publishing Co., 1988), p. 324.
13. William Hendriksen, *New Testament Commentary: Philippians* (Grand Rapids, MI: Eerdmans Publishing Co., 1962), p. 176.
14. Sinclair Ferguson, *A Heart for God* (Colorado Springs, CO: NavPress, 1985), p. 129.
15. Louis Berkhof, *Systematic Theology* (Grand Rapids, MI: Eerdmans Publishing Co., 1941), p. 52.
16. Quoted in *Gathered Gold*, p.148.

CHAPTER TWO – Where It All Begins
1. Quoted in R.C. Sproul, *Born Again: Leader Guide* (Orlando, FL: Ligonier Ministries, Inc., 1988), Chapter I, p. 14.
2. Sinclair Ferguson, *The Christian Life* (Carlisle, PA: The Banner of Truth Trust, 1989), p. 55.
3. Quoted in R.C. Sproul, *Born Again: Leader Guide*, Chapter III, p. 20.
4. C. Samuel Storms, *Chosen for Life* (Grand Rapids, MI: Baker Book House, 1987), p. 108.
5. Charles Spurgeon, *Autobiography*, 1 (Edinburgh: Banner of Truth Trust, 1962), pp. 164-65.
6. Quoted in R.C. Sproul, *Born Again: Leader Guide*, Chapter III, p. 19.
7. J.I. Packer, *God's Words* (Downers Grove, IL: InterVarsity Press, 1981), p. 151.
8. J. Rodman Williams, *Renewal Theology, Volume II: Salvation, The Holy Spirit, and Christian Living* (Grand Rapids, MI: Zondervan Publishing House, 1990), p. 37.
9. J.I. Packer, *God's Words*, pp. 148-149.
10. R.C. Sproul, *Essential Truths of the Christian Faith* (Wheaton, IL: Tyndale House, 1992), pp. 171-172.
11. Quoted in R.C. Sproul, *Born Again: Leader Guide*, Chapter III, p. 19.
12. Quoted in R.C. Sproul, *Born Again: Leader Guide*, Chapter II, p. 17.
13. J. Rodman Williams, *Renewal Theology, Volume II*, p. 50.
14. Anthony A. Hoekema, *Saved by Grace* (Grand Rapids, MI: Eerdmans Publishing Co., 1989), p. 100.
15. John R.W. Stott, *The Epistles of John* (Grand Rapids, MI: Eerdmans Publishing Co., 1964), p. 136.
16. Quoted in R.C. Sproul, *Born Again: Leader Guide*, Chapter II, p. 16.

**CHAPTER THREE – United with Christ**

1. D. Martyn Lloyd-Jones, *Romans Chapter Six: The New Man* (Grand Rapids, MI: Zondervan Publishing House, 1972), pp. 4-6.
2. John R.W. Stott, *Men Made New* (Grand Rapids, MI: Baker Book House, 1966, 1984), p. 30.
3. Lewis Smedes, *Union with Christ* (Grand Rapids, MI: Eerdmans Publishing Co., 1970; revised edition, 1983), p. xi.
4. D. Martyn Lloyd-Jones, *Romans Chapter Six*, p. 39.
5. Sinclair Ferguson, *Christian Spirituality: Five Views of Sanctification*, Donald L. Alexander, ed. (Downers Grove, IL: InterVarsity Press, 1988), p. 49.
6. Lewis Smedes, *Union with Christ*, p. 32.
7. F.F. Bruce, *The Letter of Paul to the Romans: An Introduction and Commentary* (Grand Rapids, MI: Eerdmans Publishing Co., 1985), pp. 129-130.
8. John R.W. Stott, *Men Made New*, p. 40.
9. Sinclair Ferguson, *Christian Spirituality*, p. 55.
10. D. Martyn Lloyd-Jones, *Romans Chapter Six*, p. 30.
11. F.F. Bruce, *The Letter of Paul to the Romans*, p. 132.
12. D. Martyn Lloyd-Jones, *Romans Chapter Six*, pp. 106-148 for a full discussion of these verses.
13. Jay E. Adams, *The Christian Counselor's Manual* (Grand Rapids, MI: Zondervan Publishing House, 1973), p. 118.
14. Ibid., p. 185.
15. Quoted in Sinclair Ferguson, *The Christian Life*, pp. 25-26.

**CHAPTER FOUR – The Battle Against Sin**

1. Charles J. Sykes, *A Nation of Victims: The Decay of the American Character* (New York, NY: St. Martin's Press, 1992), p. 33.
2. Ibid.
3. Franklin E. Payne, Jr., M.D., *Biblical/Medical Ethics: The Christian and the Practice of Medicine* (Milford, MI: Mott Media, Inc., 1985), p. 155.
4. William K. Kilpatrick, *Psychological Seduction: The Failure of Modern Psychology* (Nashville, TN: Thomas Nelson, Inc., 1983), p. 24.
5. J.C. Ryle, *Holiness* (Welwyn, Hertfordshire, England: Evangelical Press, 1979), p. 1.
6. J.I. Packer, *God's Words* (Downers Grove, IL: InterVarsity Press, 1981), p. 71.
7. Robert Schuller, quoted by Michael Scott Horton in *Made in America: The Shaping of Modern American Evangelicalism* (Grand Rapids, MI: Baker Book House, 1991), p. 78.
8. Quoted in Anthony A. Hoekema, *Created in God's Image* (Grand Rapids, MI: Eerdmans Publishing Co., 1986), p. 106.
9. Dan Matzat, et al., *Power Religion: The Selling Out of the Evangelical Church?*, Michael Scott Horton, ed. (Chicago, IL: Moody Press, 1992), p. 256.
10. Anthony A. Hoekema, *Saved by Grace* (Grand Rapids, MI: Eerdmans Publishing Co., 1989), p. 153.
11. Larry Crabb, *Men and Women* (Grand Rapids, MI: Zondervan Publishing House, 1991), p. 114.
12. F.F. Bruce, *The New International Commentary on the New Testament: Colossians, Philemon, and Ephesians* (Grand Rapids, MI: Eerdmans Publishing Co., 1984), p. 140.
13. Jerry Bridges, *The Practice of Godliness* (Colorado Springs, CO: NavPress, 1983), pp. 75-76.

14.Jerry Bridges, *The Pursuit of Holiness* (Colorado Springs, CO: NavPress, 1978), p. 32.

15.Quoted in Packer, *God's Words*, pp.184-185.

16.Sinclair Ferguson, *The Christian Life* (Carlisle, PA: The Banner of Truth Trust, 1989), p. 158.

17.J.I. Packer, *God's Words*, p. 182.

18.J.C. Ryle, *Holiness*, p. 55.

19.Sinclair Ferguson, *The Christian Life*, p. 162.

20.John Owen, *Temptation and Sin* (Evansville, IN: Sovereign Grace Book Club, reprint edition, 1958), p. 31.

21.Jay E. Adams, *The Christian Counselor's Manual* (Grand Rapids, MI: Zondervan Publishing House, 1973), pp. 177, 179.

22.R.C. Sproul, *The Soul's Quest for God* (Wheaton, IL: Tyndale House, 1992), p. 7.

23.J.I. Packer, *God's Words*, p. 185.

### CHAPTER FIVE – Tools of the Trade (I)

1. John Piper, *The Pleasures Of God* (Portland, OR: Multnomah Press, 1991), p. 252.

2. Anthony A. Hoekema, *Saved by Grace* (Grand Rapids, MI: Eerdmans Publishing Co., 1989), p. 29.

3. John Piper, *The Pleasures of God*, p. 56.

4. Jerry White, *The Power of Commitment* (Colorado Springs, CO: NavPress, 1985), p. 57.

5. A.W. Tozer, *Gems From Tozer* (Harrisburg, PA: Send the Light Trust/ Christian Publications, Inc., 1969), p. 4.

6. Jerry Bridges, "Declaration of Dependence" in *Discipleship Journal*, Issue 49, 1989, p. 28.

7. Quoted in Roland Bainton, *Here I Stand: A Life of Martin Luther* (Nashville, TN: Abingdon Press, 1950), p. 185.

8. Ole Christian Hallesby, *Conscience* (Minneapolis, MN: Augsburg Publishing House, 1933), p. 14.

9. J.C. Ryle, *Daily Readings From J.C. Ryle*, compiled by Robert Sheehan (Welwyn, Hertfordshire, England: Evangelical Press, 1982), p. 338.

10.Ole Christian Hallesby, *Conscience*, p. 12.

11.Jerry Bridges, *The Pursuit of Holiness* (Colorado Springs, CO: NavPress, 1978), p. 84.

12.Ole Christian Hallesby, *Conscience*, p. 144.

13.Ibid., p.142.

14.Quoted in Timothy George, *Theology of the Reformers* (Nashville, TN: Broadman Press, 1988), p. 86.

15.John Noble, *I Found God in Soviet Russia* (London: Lakeland, Marshall, Morgan & Scott, 1959)

16.Quoted in *Gathered Gold*, John Blanchard, ed. (Welwyn, Hertfordshire, England: Evangelical Press, 1984),p. 226.

### CHAPTER SIX – Tools of the Trade (II)

1. Watchman Nee, *The Release of the Spirit* (Coverdale, IN: The Sure Foundation, 1965), p. 16.

2. A.W. Tozer, *The Pursuit of God* (Camp Hill, PA: Christian Publications, Inc., 1982), pp. 22-23.

3. Walter Chantry, *The Shadow of the Cross* (Carlisle, PA: The Banner of Truth Trust, 1981), p. 7.

4. Jerry Bridges, *Transforming Grace* (Colorado Springs, CO: NavPress, 1991), p. 182.

5. D. Martyn Lloyd-Jones, *Romans 8:17-39: The Final Perseverance of*

the *Saints* (Grand Rapids, MI: Zondervan Publishing House, 1975), pp. 169-170.

6. Sinclair Ferguson, *The Christian Life* (Carlisle, PA: The Banner of Truth Trust, 1989), p. 174.
7. J.I. Packer, *Concise Theology* (Wheaton, IL: Tyndale House, 1993), p. 242.
8. Bruce Milne, *Know the Truth* (Leicester, England: InterVarsity Press, 1982), p. 153, note.
9. R.C. Sproul, "The Law of God" in *Tabletalk*, April 1989.
10. William Hendriksen, *New Testament Commentary: Galatians* (Grand Rapids, MI: Baker Book House, 1968), p. 140.
11. J.I. Packer, *The Ten Commandments* (Wheaton, IL: Tyndale House, 1977), p. 12.
12. Ibid., p. 16.
13. Anthony A. Hoekema, *Saved by Grace* (Grand Rapids, MI: Eerdmans Publishing Co., 1989), p. 225.
14. J.I. Packer, *The Ten Commandments*, pp. 17, 18.
15. John R.W. Stott, *Men Made New* (Grand Rapids, MI: Baker Book House, 1966, 1984), pp. 65-66.
16. Charles Colson and Ellen Santilli Vaughn, *The Body* (Dallas, TX: Word, Inc., 1992), p. 70.
17. David Powlison, *Dynamics of Biblical Change*, course syllabus (Laverock, PA: Christian Counseling and Educational Foundation, 1993), p. 5.
18. Sinclair Ferguson, *Christian Spirituality: Five Views of Sanctification*, Donald L. Alexander, ed. (Downers Grove, IL: InterVarsity Press, 1988), p. 74.
19. John Piper, *Desiring God* (Portland, OR: Multnomah Press, 1986), p. 66.

### CHAPTER SEVEN – Living for that Final Day
1. Darius Salter, *What Really Matters in Ministry* (Grand Rapids, MI: Baker Book House, 1990), pp. 123, 124.
2. Randy Alcorn, *Money, Possessions and Eternity* (Wheaton, IL: Tyndale House, 1989), pp. 138, 139.
3. Jerry Bridges, *Transforming Grace* (Colorado Springs, CO: NavPress, 1991), pp. 169-170.
4. Randy Alcorn, *Money, Possessions and Eternity*, p. 151.
5. Ibid.
6. J. Rodman Williams, *Renewal Theology, Volume 3: The Church, the Kingdom, and Last Things* (Grand Rapids, MI: Zondervan Publishing House, 1992), p. 457.
7. Randy Alcorn, *Money, Possessions and Eternity*, pp. 144, 149, 150-51.
8. *Jonathan Edwards—Representative Selections, with Introduction, Bibliography, and Notes*, Clarence H. Faust and Thomas H. Johnson, ed. (New York, NY: Hill and Wang, revised edition, 1962), p. 38.
9. David Powlison, "Crucial Issues in Contemporary Biblical Counseling" in *Journal of Pastoral Practice*, Vol. IX, No. 3, 1988, p. 61.
10. Randy Alcorn, *Money, Possessions and Eternity*, p. 151.
11. Ibid., p. 139.
12. Ibid., p. 137.
13. Darius Salter, *What Really Matters in Ministry*, p. 121.

### APPENDIX A – Different Roads to Holiness: An Historical Overview
1. Peter Toon, *Spiritual Companions: An Introduction to the Christian Classics* (Grand Rapids, MI: Baker Book House, 1990), p. 5.
2. Charles Kingsley, "The Hermits" in *Cyclopedia of Religious*

*Literature, Volume One* (New York, NY: John B. Alden, publisher, 1883), p. 19.

3. Peter Levi, *The Frontiers of Paradise: A Study of Monks and Monasteries* (New York, NY: Paragon House, 1987), p. 45.

4. Peter Toon, *Spiritual Companions*, pp. 5-6.

5. *Christian Spirituality: Five Views of Sanctification*, Donald L. Alexander, ed. (Downers Grove, IL: InterVarsity Press, 1988), p. 195.

6. Ibid., p. 194.

7. Peter Toon, *Spiritual Companions*, p. 6.

8. Arnold Dallimore, *George Whitefield, Volume One* (Westchester, England: Cornerstone Books, 1981), p. 186.

## APPENDIX B – The Old Man and the Flesh

1. John R.W. Stott, *Men Made New* (Grand Rapids, MI: Baker Book House, 1966, 1984), p. 45.

2. John Murray, *Principles of Conduct* (Grand Rapids, MI: Eerdmans Publishing Co., 1957), p. 218, n. 7.

3. Ibid., p. 218.

4. Ibid., p. 219.

5. Westminster Confession, XIII,2

6. John Calvin, *Institutes of the Christian Religion*, John T. McNeill, ed. (Philadelphia, PA: The Westminster Press, MCMLX), III.iii.11.

7. Heidelberg Catechism, Q. 56.

8. Anthony A. Hoekema, *Saved by Grace* (Grand Rapids, MI: Eerdmans Publishing Co., 1989), p. 213.

9. John R.W. Stott, *Men Made New*, p. 46.

# OTHER TITLES IN THE *PURSUIT OF GODLINESS* SERIES

## DISCIPLINES FOR LIFE                                    C.J. Mahaney and John Loftness

Are you satisfied with the depth of your devotional life? If you're like most Christians, probably not. *Disciplines for Life* puts change within your grasp. Leave the treadmill of spiritual drudgery behind as you discover fresh motivation and renewed passion to practice the spiritual disciplines. (96 pages)

## THIS GREAT SALVATION                                    C.J. Mahaney and Robin Boisvert

Countless Christians struggle through life feeling condemned and confused. No matter how much they do for God, they never feel quite sure of his acceptance. Sound at all familiar? Then you'll find *great* news in *This Great Salvation*. Start enjoying a new measure of grace and peace at every level of your Christian life as this unique book reveals all God has done for you through Christ. (112 pages)

## FIRST STEPS OF FAITH                                    Steve Shank

Other than a Bible, what's the first resource you would give a brand-new Christian? *First Steps of Faith* will meet that critical need. Using vivid, personal illustrations, Steve Shank lays a solid yet simple foundation for a lifetime of growth. Mature Christians will also find plenty of meat as they explore the attributes of God, our battle against indwelling sin, and much more. (112 pages)

## WHY SMALL GROUPS?                                    C.J. Mahaney, General Editor

Not simply a how-to guide, this illuminating book starts by answering the all-important question of *why* a church needs small groups. The short answer? Because small groups are invaluable in helping us to "work out our salvation together" in practical, biblical ways. Specially developed for leaders and members of small groups alike, *Why Small Groups?* is loaded with insight, wisdom, and practical instruction. This book can help put you on the fast track to Christian maturity. (128 pages)

## THE RICH SINGLE LIFE                    Andrew Farmer, foreword by Joshua Harris

How do you live your life as a Christian single? Are you aiming at something better than just continually coping? God intends the season of your singleness to be one of great richness, focus, and fulfillment in him—a time when abundance joins hands with opportunity, and your identity in Christ emerges from undivided devotion to the Lord. While acknowledging the unique challenges the single life can pose, this book applies the truth and the heart of the Scripture in a way that is inspiring, encouraging, and practical. (176 pages)

# ADDITIONAL RESOURCES FROM SOVEREIGN GRACE MINISTRIES

## WORSHIP MUSIC

Since 1982, our ministry has published more than 300 songs, written by men and women in our family of churches, and intended to assist Christians in their worship of God. After several releases with major Christian labels, we began the Come & Worship series in 1997 (under our former name, PDI Music) as our primary means of releasing new songs to the Body of Christ. That mission continues under the new name of Sovereign Grace Music (effective September, 2002).

*"Singing and knowing. Rejoicing and reasoning. Delight and doctrine. That's Sovereign Grace! It is so rare, and so needed … So sing on, Sovereign Grace! And whatever you do, don't stop studying and thinking and preaching about our great Savior."* — **author and pastor John Piper**

*"These songs are vital, rich, and heart-probing ... [Sovereign Grace] music moves my heart to worship."* — **Randy Alcorn, author of** Safely Home, Edge of Eternity, Deadline, Dominion, *and* Money, Possessions & Eternity

*"I grew up in church. I grew up singing praise songs. But honestly, I didn't learn to worship until I encountered songs like the ones from Sovereign Grace. Great music? Yes, but better yet, great truth. They're rooted in God's word, anchored to the cross, drenched in grace. They're the kinds of songs our generation is longing for—songs that exalt God, songs that leave us standing in awe of Him."* — **Joshua Harris, author of** I Kissed Dating Goodbye, Boy Meets Girl, *and* Not Even a Hint

## AUDIO MESSAGES

Sovereign Grace produces audio series on a number of topics, ideal for personal and small-group application. Thousands have been evangelized, exhorted, encouraged, and instructed by these messages, first presented in local churches or at conferences such as the various Sovereign Grace conferences for pastors, worship leaders and worship teams, small-group leaders, and others. At the teaching section of our website you can review outlines to many of these messages (www.sovereigngraceministries.org/teaching). These products are available in CD and audiocassette formats.

**For more information, please visit www.sovereigngraceministries.org**
**To order from the Sovereign Grace Store, visit www.sovereigngracestore.com**

**Sovereign Grace Ministries**
**7505 Muncaster Mill Road**
**Gaithersburg, MD 20877**
**info@sovgracemin.org**
**301-330-7400**